BEYOND THE IMAGE

On Visual Culture

in the Twenty-First Century

Alessandro Sbordoni

A Set Margins' publication

"They have offended the thing I hold most dear: my image."

— Silvio Berlusconi

Warning

Two centuries ago, at the beginning of the technological revolution, Friedrich Nietzsche wrote: "What I relate is the history of the next two centuries. I describe what is coming, what can no longer come differently: the *advent of nihilism*. This history can be related even now; for necessity itself is at work here."[1] While he was scrawling these notes between 1887 and 1888, his ears were perfectly tuned to the sound of the twenty-first century: "This future speaks even now in a hundred signs, [...] for this music of the future all ears are cocked."[2] Yet, at the same time, he was also an increasingly short-sighted philologist who did not see the shapes that were reproduced before his own eyes: lithography, photography, and electric light were all technologies that had been invented or developed in the nineteenth century.

Two centuries after Friedrich Nietzsche's warning, the future of the image is reproduced in a thousand, a million, even a trillion signs. From deepfakes to computer-generated imagery, from shitposting to dank memes: the uppermost value of the image devalues itself. *Nihilism is trending right now*. As the number of images increases, they are like a *stream*, to repurpose a phrase by the German philologist; they run fiercely toward their end but do not reflect any sunlight.

1. Friedrich Nietzsche, *The Will to Power*, tr. Walter Kaufmann and R. J. Hollingdale, New York: Vintage, 1968, p. 3.
2. Friedrich Nietzsche, *The Will to Power*, p. 3.

As soon as analog technology shifts to digital technology, reproduction supersedes the archaic principle of representation. In the twenty-first century, there are no more values except those set by the market. This is the disvaluation of the image in the third millennium that Friedrich Nietzsche's prophecy *overlooked*.

The devaluation of the image is also the beginning of its revaluation. 2087-2088: *save the date*!

THIS IS THE STORY OF THE IMAGE OF THE TWENTY-FIRST CENTURY

In his *Natural History*, Pliny the Elder tells the myth of Zeuxis and Parrhasius, the best painters of the classical age.[3] When the two challenged each other in an artistic contest, Zeuxis painted a bunch of grapes so realistically that the birds flew over to peck at it. Meanwhile, Parrhasius presented only the image of a curtain. "And now, show me your painting," said Zeuxis. But there was nothing behind the veil. Zeuxis deceived the birds, but Parrhasius beguiled the eyes of another artist.

Today, we no longer believe in images. "We no longer believe the truth remains truth," as Friedrich Nietzsche writes, "when the veils are withdrawn."[4] Two hundred years after the first photograph by Nicéphore Niépce, images do not designate any reality whatsoever. In the twenty-first century, reality is no longer the *default* principle of the image. This incredulity is, in part, the product of technology.

There is an image of Samuel Beckett and King Bowser, the antagonist of the *Super Mario* franchise. The photograph was taken in Japan at the release party for the video game *Super Mario Bros 2*, in 1988, only a year before Samuel Beckett's death. The author of *Waiting for Godot* and Endgame was popular in Japan and wanted to endorse the new video game. The black-and-white photograph was posted on X by Gabriel Smith (@gabriel666smith) on November 20th, 2023. Except that the image was a deepfake created using artificial intelligence. *The "truth" is that there is nothing true*

[3] Pliny the Elder, *Natural History*, Book XXXV, tr. Harris Rackman, Cambridge: Loeb, 1938.

[4] Friedrich Nietzsche, *Gay Science: With a Prelude in Rhymes and an appendix of Songs*, tr. Walter Kaufmann, London: Vintage, 1974, p. 38.

WE DO NOT BELIEVE IN IMAGES ANYMORE

FIGURE 1. Samuel Beckett and King Bowser

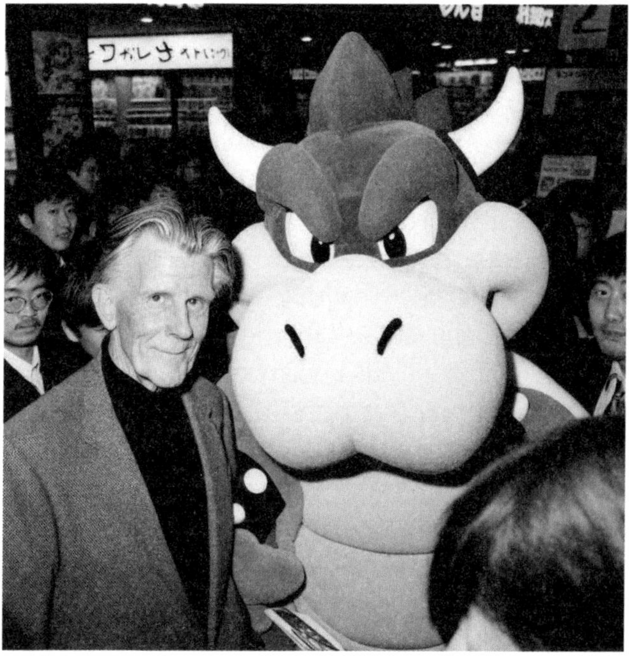

Images do not designate any reality.
This incredulity is, in part, the product of technology.

in the image. This image is part of the world of ideas, as Jacques Lacan writes with regard to the story of Zeuxis and Parrhasius, rather than the world of senses; the image does not compete with appearance but with what is always beyond appearance.[5]

"What color is that dress? I see white & gold. Kanye sees black & blue, who is color blind?"[6] tweeted Kim Kardashian (@KimKardashian) in 2015. Within a week since the picture of the dress was originally posted on Facebook by a Scottish woman, more than ten million users replied to the same question on Twitter. But the question (#TheDress) was *never* about the color of the real garment. It was only about *the tinge of the image.* Two minutes after Kim Kardashian's tweet, BuzzFeed comments: "Apparently it's black and blue."[7] The fault of BuzzFeed, in analogy with Zeuxis, is to believe that reality was still the *default* of the image.
The mirror, whose physics defined the principle of the image for millennia, is superseded by the screen.
In the twenty-first century, the format of the image is no longer reflecting and transcendent but, on the contrary, immanent and transparent. On the one hand, the mirror-image is the *double.* "Avert your gaze and you will lose your love, / for this that holds your eyes is nothing save / the image of yourself reflected back to you,"[8] writes Ovid in the tale of Narcissus and Echo. The screen-image, on the other hand, is the sign of the

5 Jacques Lacan, *Seminar XI: The Four Fundamental Concepts of Psychoanalysis*, tr. Alan Sheridan, New York - London: W. W. Norton, 1998, p. 112.
6 Kim Kardashian, What Color Is that Dress?, *X [Twitter]*, 27 February 2015, available at https://x.com/kimkardashian/status/571168149871177730.
7 BuzzFeed, @KimKardashian Apparently It's Black and Blue, *X [Twitter]*, 27 February 2015, available at https://x.com/BuzzFeed/status/571168834092199936.

THE "TRUTH" IS THAT THERE IS NOTHING TRUE IN THE IMAGE

self-same.
In 2010, Paris Hilton and Britney Spears "invented" the selfie with a BlackBerry cellphone. In contrast with the mirror of René Magritte's painting *Not to Be Reproduced*, where a man (the artist's patron, Edward James) looks inside the glass and sees only the back of his head, Paris Hilton and Britney Spears look at the cellphone only to see the front of their heads, over and over again. The image of the other is replaced by the image of the self-same.
If the mirror stage ends with the identification of the double,[9] the screen stage *never* ends because the image is always-already identical to itself. In logical contraposition to the mirror, the screen is not a reflecting and transcendent surface but a transparent and immanent one. The psychological drama returns as a technological farce.

In Yayoi Kusama's artwork *Infinity Mirrored Room*, the image of the viewer is reflected in all directions by the mirrors on the four walls, the floor, and the ceiling. Notwithstanding, the viewer never sees the mirrors as such. In fact, the mirrors inside the art installation are viewed, for the first and last time, through the lens of the viewer's screen. The mirrored images refract only into an infinite series of selfies (hashtags #YayoiKusama and #InfinityMirroredRoom). The mirror images of the viewer are repeated to infinity, only to be looked at from yet another screen...
In the age of electronic reproduction, the more an

8 Ovid, *Metamorphoses*, tr. Brookes More, Boston: Cornhill Publishing Co., 1922, p. 407.
9 Jacques Lacan, *Écrits*, tr. Alan Sheridan, London - New York: Routledge, 2001.

artwork is reproduced, the more it is valuable.[10] It is according to this formula that *scarcity* is supplanted by the *profusion* of signs. The value of Yayoi Kusama's *Infinity Mirrored Room* is proportional to its reproducibility as an image: its Instagrammability. The image only dissimulates the fact that there is nothing else to see beyond it except more and more images. *Take a selfie!*

It is not possible to go through the looking glass anymore. Transcendence is replaced by immanence. The value of the artwork is no longer opaque: it is transparent, just like the medium through which it is priced and sold.

Theory, whose primary meaning in ancient Greek is *look, show, spectacle,* and even *a feast for the eye*, has always been in a relationship with vision, whose metaphors have, in turn, shaped the values of truth, beauty, and morality in Western culture.[11] In other words, theory sharpens the tools by means of which images are reproduced in a circle.

In the nineteenth and early twentieth century, the economy itself takes the place of the metaphor of the circle: the images reproduce again and again and again by means of technology. Reproduction is the new factory setting. Representation is a principle that no longer explains the image and its technology away. The theoretical spectacle is overcome by the technical one. The question of theorists like Walter Benjamin is, in this regard, only about the format of their own spectacle after the technics of lithography and photography.[12]

10 McKenzie Wark, My Collectible Ass, *e-flux, 85*, 2017, available at https://www.e-flux.com/journal/85/156418/my-collectible ass/.

11 George Lakoff and Mark Johnson, *Metaphors We Live By*, Chicago - London: University of Chicago Press, 1980.

THE MORE AN ARTWORK IS REPRODUCED, THE MORE IT IS VALUABLE

In the late twentieth century, the circular logic of the image has superseded the linear logic of text. If the end of capitalism is always beginning and never ending, it is not just a post-modernist *figure of speech*... The image, in contrast with the word, is without any beginning or end: its logic is not linear but circular. After the end of history - that is, after the end of the linear time of writing -, there is always another figure. The struggle that today takes place between the linear and irreversible structure of the text against the circular and reversible structure of the image, which started in the ancient era with the Jewish prophets and ancient Greek philosophers, in particular Plato, is inverted once again.[13] On the one hand, image technology is the product of applied theory. On the other hand, as more and more images are reproduced, language is only about the stream of images (in the form of posts, comments, reviews) and, in a circle, it is a second-order simulation of their value.
The revolution of the image is inexorable; it is already turning its screw into the capitalist machine.

In the nineteenth century, Stephan Mallarmé writes: "Everything in the world exists to end up as a book." [14] In the twentieth century, Susan Sontag revises: "Everything exists to end in a photograph." [15] In the twenty-first century, everything in the world exists in order to end up as an image file. A trillion images

12 For more, Friedrich Kittler, *Optical Media: Berlin Lectures 1999*, tr. Anthony Enns, Cambridge: Polity, 2010 and Walter Benjamin, *The Work of Art in the Age of Mechanical Reproduction*, tr. J. A. Underwood, London: Penguin, 2008.

13 Vilém Flusser, *Towards a Philosophy of Photography*, tr. Anthony Mathews, London: Reaktion, 2006.

14 Stephan Mallarmé, Le Livre, Instrument Spirituel [The Book as Spiritual Instrument], as cited in Stephan Mallarmé, *The Book*, tr. Sylvia Gorelick, Cambridge: Exact Change, 2018, p. v.

15 Susan Sontag, *On Photography*, Middlesex: Penguin, 1977, p. 19

are reproduced every day: more than the number of galaxies in the universe. Like in a Borges story,[16] the images are not destroyed for fear that the world itself would end with them. They are only stored away in the hard drive.
The digital archive is qualitatively different from the analog archive in one respect: *quantity.* Each year, the capacity of the hard drive increases exponentially according to Moore's law, as formulated by Intel co-founder Gordon Moore in 1965.[17] The *corollary* of the law is that the quantity of images increases accordingly. In 2024, when *brain rot* was named as the Word of the Year by the Oxford English Dictionary, the number of transistors per chip was more than 10^{11}.
Landfills are increasingly stuffed with electronic waste while the Internet is filled with more and more garbage.

Trash culture is a product of the shift from analog to digital technology. It is only the most *logical* result of technological progress.
Trash in the twenty-first century is fast (and faster every other year). Kitsch in the twentieth and nineteenth centuries is slow. Kitsch is the *Mona Lisa* printed on an apron. Trash is Pepe the Frog. The old kitsch is local. The new trash is global.
The art critic Clement Greenberg writes: "Kitsch is a product of the industrial revolution [...]. The peasants

16 Jorge Luis Borges, *The Book of Sand*, tr. Norman Thomas di Giovanni, New York: E. P. Dutton, 1977.
17 Gordon Moore, Cramming More Components onto Integrated Circuits, *Electronics Magazine, 38(8)*, 19 April 1965.

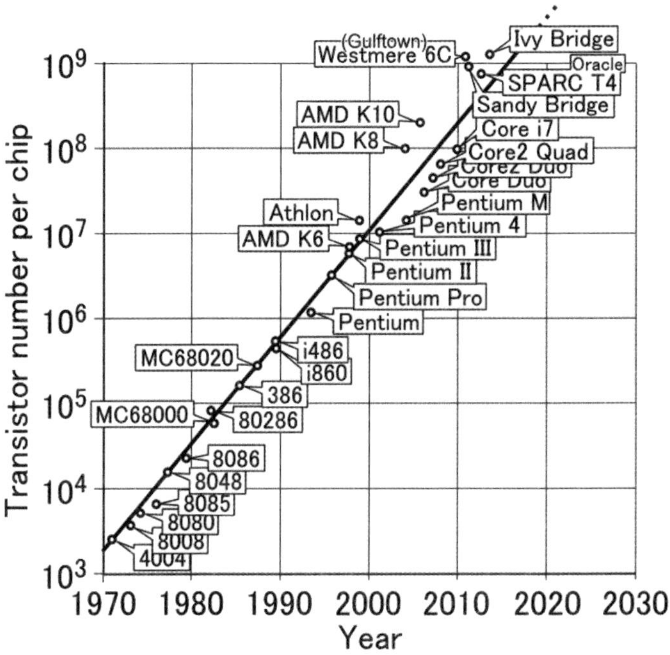

Every year, the capacity of the hard drive increases exponwentially according to Moore's law. The corollary is that the quantity of images increases accordingly.

who settled in the cities as proletariat and petty bourgeois [...] [losing] their taste for the folk culture whose background was the countryside, and discovering a new capacity for boredom at the same time, the new urban masses set up a pressure on society to provide them with a kind of culture fit for their own consumption."[18] Trash, too, is a product of the industrial revolution: the *third* one. It is the artifact of the information age. Trash is the culture of the World Wide Web. If kitsch is the culture of the working class, trash is for everybody.

I asked ChatGPT: "Who is the *trashiest* artist today?" Answer: "Damien Hirst." A few years ago, the British artist destroyed some paintings from his series *The Currency* on a live stream, following their sale as NFTs. As soon as they were sold, they were no longer useful as images: they were only junk.

Kitsch and trash overlap. Nevertheless, the main difference is that, while kitsch is the servant's copy of the master's original artwork, trash *junks* the distinction between high and low culture, avant-garde and rear-garde, expensive original and cheap copy. For example, the digital rendition of the *Nyan Cat* meme, a YouTube video from 2011, was sold ten years later for about $600,000 (while Marcel Duchamp's reproduction of the *Mona Lisa* with a mustache was sold at an auction for €600,000). If kitsch is nostalgic about "the great art of the past," trash is only nostalgic about the great artifice of reality. If kitsch is political, as Boris Groys argues,[19] trash is always *beyond* politics (and in this regard, it is even more political). Andy Warhol: kitsch. The Kardashians: trash.

For more than two hundred years, the function of the

18 Clement Greenberg, *Art and Culture: Critical Essays*, Boston: Beacon Press, 1989, pp. 9 - 10.

19 Boris Groys, *In the Flow*, London - New York: Verso, 2016.

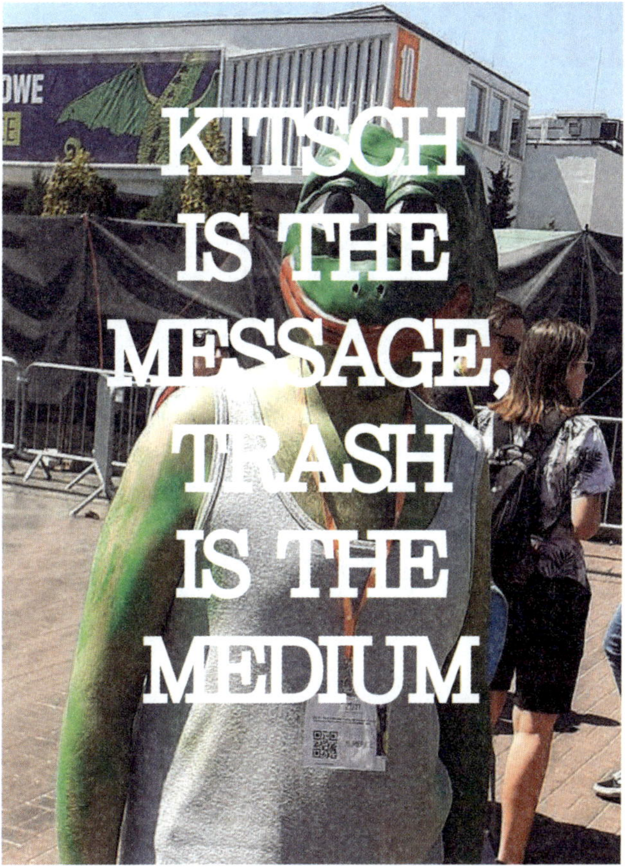

FIGURE 3. Pepe the Frog

IT IS EASIER
TO IMAGINE
THE END OF
THE WORLD
THAN THE
END OF TRASH

image has been to entertain. "A capitalist society requires a culture based on images. It needs to furnish vast amounts of entertainment," writes Susan Sontag, "in order to stimulate buying and anesthetize the injuries of class, race, and sex." [20]

The image is functional to the reproduction of the system of production. The image is part of the *reproduction* of the labor force, in the guise of the consumer. But while the imagery is free, the viewer is the product. In the third millennium, the reproductive labor reserved for women, such as taking care of infants and elders at little or no cost, [21] is taken over by the screen.

Since the reproduction of the image itself is profitable, the difference between work and leisure is trashed. From young to old, the image is shown only for the sake of capital. Watch a dozen videos on children's YouTube and the short animation of a little happy train is followed, twelve clicks later, by an erotic fan art of Mickey Mouse.[22] The function of the image as such is no longer to entertain but, above all, to generate revenue.

Julius Klinger, one of the pioneers of modern advertising, once argued that, counter to the artistic trend of the image that is, by default, without finality, at least

20 Susan Sontag, *On Photography*, Middlesex: Penguin, 1977, p. 178.

21 For more, Silvia Federici, *Revolution at Point Zero: Housework, Reproduction, and Feminist Struggle*, Oakland: PM Press, 2012.

22 James Bridle, The Nightmare Videos of Childrens' YouTube - and What's Wrong with the Internet Today, April 2018, *Ted*, available at https://www.ted.com/talks/james_bridle_the_nightmare_videos_ of_children_s_youtube_and_what_s_wrong_with_the_internet_today/ reading-list and James Bridle, *New Dark Age: Technology and the Future*, London - Brooklyn: Verso, 2018.

FIGURE 4. Garbage dump

the commercial image has an end: to sell.[23] Aesthetics is replaced by economics. In the twenty-first century, advertising no longer functions as an image; the image functions as advertising. Even the AI-generated picture of Samuel Beckett and King Bowser, cited at the begin ning of this book, was used to advertise Gabriel Smith's upcoming book, entitled *Brat: A Ghost Story*. As the capitalist system reproduces itself inside the imagery, *the stare intensifies*.

"You don't own a TV? What's all your furniture pointed at?" [24] (Joey Tribbiani in *Friends*). In the early twenty-first century, the television set was the center of the hearth. It was the point around which the living room was designed: the armchair, the lamp, the table. The living room, in the interior design of *Friends*, was synonymous with the TV room. It was more than a home appliance. Television was the center of the *gaze*. As soon as the stationary screen shifts to a mobile one, it is more and more like a sphere whose center is everywhere and whose circumference is nowhere.
If big and small screens reproduce the male gaze, in which man is the bearer of the look and woman is nothing more than an image,[25] the screens reproduce only the eyes of the consumer. The gaze is replaced by the stare. In contrast with the former, the latter is always-already *centered on the device*. The stare is less and less a psychological complex and more and more a

23 Adolfo Conti (dir.), *Plakat: The Birth of Modern Advertising*, ARTE, 2018.
24 Kevin S. Bright (dir.), *Friends*, Season 9, Episode 23, NBC, 2003.
25 Laura Mulvey, Visual Pleasure and Narrative Cinema, in Leo Braudy and Marshall Cohen (eds), *Film Theory and Criticism: Introductory Readings* (pp. 833 - 844), New York: Oxford University Press, 1999.

THE STARE INTENSIFIES

technological one.
In the twentieth century, the machine automated the hands of workers; in the twenty-first century, it automates the eyes of consumers. *The conveyor belt is upgraded by scrolling.* Every image is reproduced as the umpteenth sign of consumption. It is the fantasy of capitalism itself for the image. The eye as such is put in the service of capital. For example, when users watch content on social media platforms like TikTok, the recommendation algorithm searches for the next video to play. When customers shop for a product on the Shein website, the online platform uses the customer data to design the next item to upload.[26] *If you liked this veil, you will love the next one.*
In contrast with the analog medium, whose audience is overall general and non-discrete, the digital image is advertised to an audience that is specific and discrete. As soon as the gaze is quantifiable and measurable (for example, how much time did you stare at this picture? How much time did you *not* stare?), the image is custom-made for the consumer.

"For 50 years, heroin addicts have used methadone to help break their addiction. Now you can step down your dependency on your mobile device with this: *methaphone*. Leave your phone without the cravings or withdrawal," as the product description of an acrylic slab shaped like a smartphone reads. "We carry our phones everywhere. It feels strange and unsettling when we can't feel them. We twitch, worried we've lost something. methaphone can help you manage cravings and withdrawal symptoms. It can fill that hole in your back pocket. It can fill that hole in your hand.

26 The Wall Street Journal, How Shein Built a $66B Fast-Fashion Empire WSJ The Economics Of, *YouTube*, 29 November 2023, available at https://www.youtube.com/watch?v=gWotBPtsulo.

CLICK HERE
TO VIEW
MORE

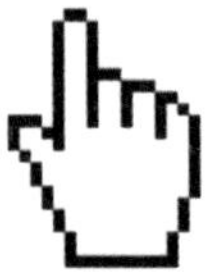

FIGURE 5. Hand cursor

Opioid addicts have used methadone to help step down from dependency, and now you have this." [27]

In the third millennium, digital detox is the equivalent of allotherapy for a new type of cancer. As Big Tobacco is the main promoter of anti-smoking campaigns, Big Tech and its ideologues are the main sponsors for limited screen time. The medium of the image, to use a Baudrillardian analogy, is metastatic (or *methastatic*). It reproduces beyond its own end.

"Six hours less radio in Indonesia next week," [28] wrote Marshall McLuhan in 1964 or "five hours less of TV in Italy," [29] he said in 1969, to heat up the medium - as Indonesians and Italians switch to books and newspapers - and rehabilitate, albeit temporarily, the sense and sensibility of the subjects. Nevertheless, four hours less of digital technology, in a system in which images are an *integral part* of so-called reality, is not enough. Forget about Internet-addiction camps in South Korea and digital detox in Finland... *There is a new message for you*: it is from *capitalism*.

The metastasis is at its last stage. The medium is cancerous not only at the level of reproduction, but production itself. "We need to recalibrate the image and our eyes," [30] remark Mieke Gerritzen and Geert Lovink in their 2019 *Design Manifesto*. Instead of digital detox, another modus operandi is designed from a new

27 Mindless Toys, *methaphone*, 2025, available at https://mindless-toys.com/products/methaphone-a-mobile-detox-device.

28 Marshall McLuhan, *Understanding Media: The Extensions of Man*, London - New York: Ark, 1987, p. 28.

29 Marshall McLuhan, Playboy Interview: "Marshall McLuhan—A Candid Conversation with the High Priest of Popcult and Metaphysician of Media", in Eric McLuhan and Frank Zingrone (eds) *Essential McLuhan* (222 - 260), London: Routledge, 2005, pp. 254 - 255.

30 Mieke Gerritzen and Geert Lovink, *Made in China, Designed in California, Criticised in Europe*: Amsterdam Design Manifesto, Amsterdam: BIS, 2019, p. 28.

relationship with technology as such. "DEALING WITH THE PUMP & DUMP SELF," the two theorists write in all caps next to the statement "IF YOU DON'T KNOW WHAT TO DO, CREATE A NEW SELF."[31] The function of the image is overturned.

Two centuries before Friedrich Nietzsche's *The Wanderer and His Shadow*, René Descartes wrote about a blind man who "through the medium of a stick" is able to see with his hands rather than his eyes. The blind man's stick, he wrote, "is the organ of some sixth sense given to [him] in place of sight."[32] In analogy, light itself "passes toward our eyes through the medium of the air and other transparent bodies, in the same manner that the movement or resistance of the bodies that this blind man encounters is transmitted to his hand through the medium of his stick."[33] Thus, the Cartesian blind man is able to *see* the difference between the trees, stones, sand, water, grass, and mud by means of his cane, just like the scientist is able to perceive each image apart from the other through vision. In both instances, the optical metaphor is not only a way of seeing but a *worldview* according to which seeing is always-already equal to understanding.
Even if the analogy is not true - *verbatim*: "there is a great difference between the stick of this blind man and the air or the other transparent bodies through the medium of which we see"[34] -, it is according to the logic behind it that Descartes then cuts his lenses and makes the technology which, in turn, allow him

31 Mieke Gerritzen and Geert Lovink, *Made in China, Designed in California, Criticised in Europe*, p. 92.
32 René Descartes, Optics, in *Discourse on Method, Optics, Geometry, and Meteorology* (pp. 65 - 176), tr. Paul J. Olscamp, Indianapolis - Cambridge: Hackett, 2001, p. 67.
33 René Descartes, Optics, p. 67.
34 René Descartes, Optics, pp. 68 - 69.

to reproduce what he sees into yet another image. While optics ministers to the deficiencies of vision by means of "artificial organs" to correct the defects of short-sighted and long-sighted eyes with corneal lenses, it does not remediate the "natural organs" through which it looks at technics itself. In fact, it is only by analogy with a *camera obscura* that René Descartes is able to explain the reversal of the images that form on the back of the eye.

There is a quote from one of Jean Baudrillard's books on Goodreads that goes like this: "The media represents a world that is more real than reality that we can experience. People lose the ability to distinguish between reality and fantasy. They also begin to engage with the fantasy without realizing what it really is [...]. (Note: This quote is fake and does not appear in *Simulacra and Simulation*. I tried to delete it, but the system doesn't allow that because this quote has 'too many fans' lol.)" [35] The quote itself is not real. Nevertheless, it reproduces itself (it is *liked* and shared) by means of its own hyperreality: the principle is not representation but reproduction. As analog technology shifts to digital technology, the principle of reality also changes accordingly.
When Spider-Man first appears in the Marvel Cinematic Universe, it is only a computer-generated image of the superhero. Tom Holland, the actor who plays Peter Parker in *Captain America: Civil War*, was not even cast yet. In fact, it is only in retrospect that the

35 Goodreads, "The Media Represents a World that Is More Real than Reality", *Goodreads*, available at https://www.goodreads.com/quotes/7417476-the-media-represents-world-that-is-more-real-than-reality.

FIGURE 6. iPhone 8

This is not a screen

superhero looks like Tom Holland. The last stage of the motion picture has no relation to reality whatsoever, reality itself is only a special effect of the virtual, which is then edited in post-production. The image is no longer part of the order of appearance but the order of simulation. To quote Spider-Man himself: "That thing doesn't obey the laws of physics at all!" [36] The reality principle of the image is scrapped. The staged images of Spider-Man do away with true and false appearances altogether. "They're crap. Crap, crap, megacrap. I'll give you two hundred bucks for all of 'em" [37] (J. Jonah Jameson in the first film of the *Spider-Man* trilogy). Tom Holland, in this regard, is not paid to star as Peter Parker but to dissimulate the fact that there is nothing beside the computer-generated imagery.
When Charlie Chaplin participated in a Charlot look-alike contest, he only won the third prize. But when, more than one hundred years later, Timothée Chalamet went to his own look-alike competition, the event itself no longer looked real (as a matter of fact, it was a promotional stunt to advertise the YouTube channel of Anthony Potero, the artist who organized the event). It is when the image is the most realistic that it no longer acts like a mirror but like a screen, beyond which there is nothing else to view. It is when the image is the most realistic, that reality itself is disqualified from any contest.
Reality has lost its own mirror image. In a Baudrillardian fashion, Tom Holland and Timothée Chalamet cannot jump over their shadows because they no longer have any.

When "the medium is the message," to use Marshall

36 Anthony Russo and Joe Russo (dir.), *Captain America: Civil War*, Marvel Studios, 2016.
37 Sam Raimi (dir.), *Spider-Man*, Sony, 2002.

McLuhan's phrase, there is also no message.[38]
When Kanye West's wife Bianca Censori walked on the Grammy's red carpet, she only wore a fur coat on top of a transparent dress. When she removed the coat, the cameras covered her naked body with an opaque filter. As soon as you watch the photograph of Bianca Censori, you are always-already staring at the screen. Like the veil of Parrhasius, the image no longer hides the fact that there is nothing else to see. The veils are withdrawn. There is no truth as such anymore.
In Dante's *Vita Nova*, where the Italian word for screen makes its first-ever appearance, the screen to the truth ("schermo de la veridade") is literally a woman who stands between the eyes of Dante and his beloved Beatrice. Dante watches the screen in order to look at Beatrice.[39] The screen, at the same time, blocks and reveals what is behind it. On the other hand, there is nothing behind Bianca Censori's screen-out. Kanye West, like Dante, feigns his love only to stare at the screen (and be watched by means of it).

In 2021, someone paid $650,000 for a yacht that exists only in The Sandbox metaverse. In contrast with any real yacht, the "Metaflower Super Mega Yacht" is only useful as money and no longer as a boat. But then, it is the yacht *par excellence*: it is just an asset within a portfolio. Ironically, when every image is possible, the only imagery that is reproduced is that of capital.

38 Marshall McLuhan and Quentin Fiore, *The Medium Is the Massage: An Inventory of Effects*, London: Penguin, 1967. For more, Jean Baudrillard, *In the Shadow of the Silent Majorities or, The End of the Social and Other Essays*, tr. Paul Foss, Paul Patton, and John Johnston, Los Angeles: Semiotext(e), 1983.

39 Dante, *The New Life*, tr. Dante Gabriel Rossetti, London: Ellis and Elvey, 1899.

FIGURE 7. Salmon prompt

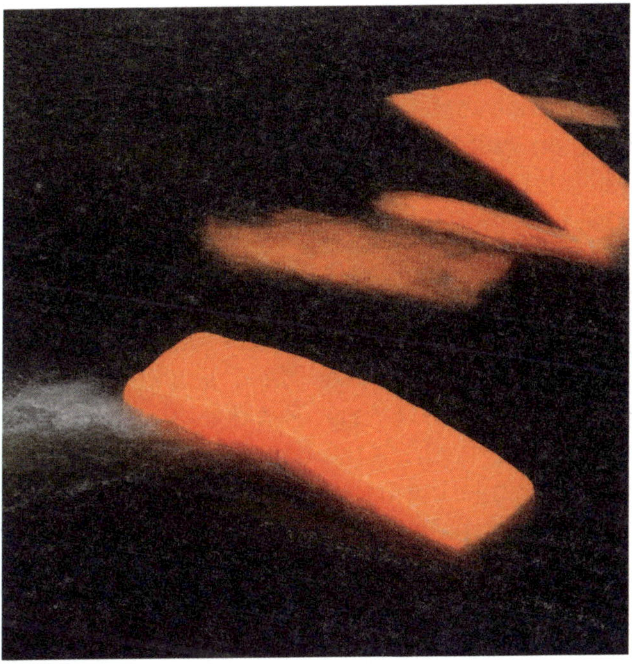

"Whatever stands by in the sense of standing-reserve no longer stands over against us as object." [40]

– Martin Heidegger

[40] Martin Heidegger, *The Question Concerning Technology*, p. 17.

When the text prompt "salmon swimming in the river" is generated as an image by artificial intelligence, the salmon pic is not a living animal but a fish steak in a stream of water. The text-to-image prompt is neither true nor false. Instead, it is only the *standing-reserve* of consumption (*Bestand* in Heideggerian terminology).[41] Image and data become indistinguishable. As the forester "who, in the wood, measures the felled timber and to all appearances walks the same forest path in the same way as did his grandfather[, but he] is today commanded by profit-making in the lumber industry, whether he knows it or not,"[42] the image of the "salmon swimming in the river" is, too, just the sign of the industry. The salmon swims upstream only in order to reproduce itself as yet another picture. The image no longer *represents* truth but, on the contrary, *reproduces* itself according to the logic of reversibility. As Angelicism01 writes in a re-translation of Martin Heidegger's essay *The Turn*: "The Internet comes online as the danger. But does the danger therewith announce itself as the danger? No. [...] the danger, namely, endangering itself in the truth of its coming to be online, remains veiled and disguised. This disguising and 'coping' is what is most dangerous in the danger."[43]

Dasein is updated by design. The format of the image takes precedence over the word. *It's giving...* is a slang phrase used by Zoomers to describe the vibe of an image, just like in Martin Heidegger's language *es*

41 Martin Heidegger, *The Question Concerning Technology*, tr. William Lovitt, New York-London: Harper & Row, 1977.
42 Martin Heidegger, *The Question Concerning Technology*, p. 18.
43 Angelicism01, Heidegger on NFTs: A 'Translation' by Angelicism01 RIP. From The Turning, *Substack*, 4 March 2021, available at https://ia800603.us.archive.org/35/items/angelicism01-email-archive/20210403-HEIDEGGER%20ON%20NFTS-221.txt.

gibt... (literally, *it gives*) is always the signifier of a mood. The vibe, however, in contrast with the mood or the emotional disposition, is not about *what* something is; it is about *how* something is.
Dasein is represented in the mood of anxiety. On the other hand, bad vibes are engineered on social media platforms only to reproduce more capital. Look at how any image is reproduced: *it's giving... capitalism*. The vibes are off.
But what is *it* that *it's giving...*? None other than the framework in which the image is reproduced. Indeed, the vibe is less and less a relation between the viewer and the image than between the viewer and the medium. An Internet vibe, for example, is only the relation with the global scale of culture. There is no distinction, in technological terms, between good and bad feels. There are only images that are reproduced faster than others: *vibez*.

The CAPTCHA, short for Completely Automated Public Turing test to tell Computers and Humans Apart, was first invented to deter bot attacks by requiring users to identify the presence of a specific item: for example, to select all images with boats in them. But now, the same test is used, in turn, to train the bots that it tried to deter. The CAPTCHA user is part of a feedback system between one machine and another piece of machinery.
Then, the viewer of the CAPTCHA is, literally, estranged from his own gaze. Each image only refers to other images, which, in turn, are deferred to more images. The epistemics of truth is replaced by the auto-verification of the image. The image is neither true nor false, only correct or incorrect.
Now, the same logic is used by ImageNet and other

SELECT ALL SQUARES WITH REALITY

IF THERE IS NONE, CLICK "SKIP"

large image databases and scaled up to label millions and millions of pictures. ImageNet clickworkers viewed one image per second on average: for example, "Are there any *grapes* in this picture?" Then, there are no images any longer, only more boxes to tick.

The image of production disappears in the name of the reproduction of the image. In fact, it was only when the immaterial labor of the ImageNet project was crowdsourced to Amazon's Mechanical Turk-which paid its piecemeal workers less than a cent to label each image-that the ImageNet project was able to become the largest image database at the time (as well as the largest academic user of Amazon's Mechanical Turk).[44]

The economics of the image replaces its epistemics. The bias towards capital reproduces at the same time as its racist, sexist, and colonialist algorithm. In 2019, ImageNet Roulette, an art project by Kate Crawford and Trevor Paglen, enabled anyone to upload a picture to ImageNet's database and see how the algorithm labeled their images according to its 2,833 subcategories. Some users were categorized as "slattern, slut, slovenly woman, trollop," "alcoholic, alky, dipsomaniac, boozer, lush, soaker, souse," or labeled by the algorithm with other slurs;[45] for instance, a technology reporter from The Guardian was only a "gook."[46]

44 For more, Kate Crawford, *Atlas of AI: Power, Politics, and the Planetary Costs of Artificial Intelligence*, New Haven - London: Yale University Press, 2021.

45 Kate Crawford and Trevor Paglen, Excavating AI: The Politics of Images in *Machine Learning Training Sets, Excavating AI*, 19 September 2019, available at https://excavating.ai/.

46 Julia Carrie Wong, The Viral Selfie App ImageNet Roulette Seemed Fun - Until it Called Me a Racist Slur, *The Guardian*, 18 September 2019, available at https://www.theguardian.com/technology/2019/ sep/17/imagenet-roulette-asian-racist-slur-selfie.

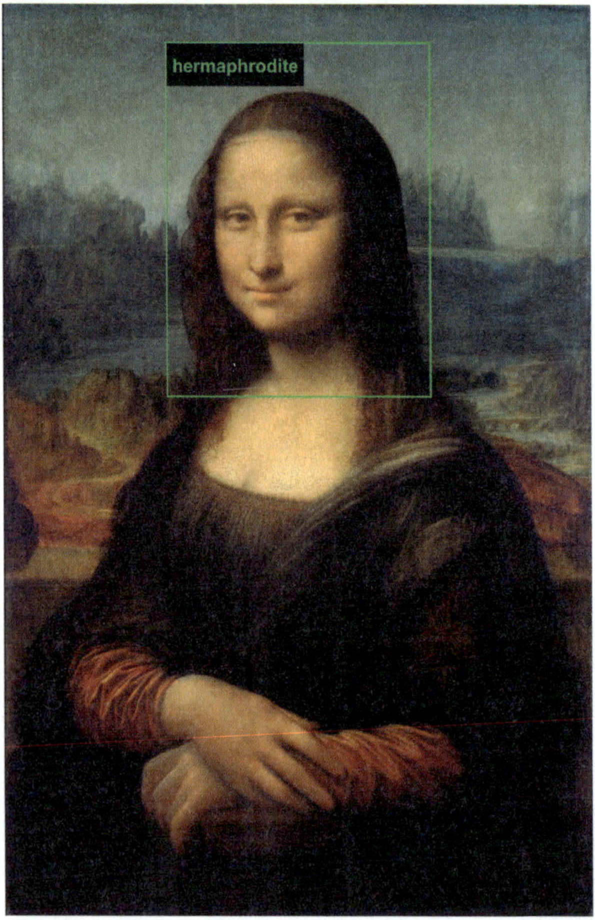

FIGURE 8. *Mona Lisa* with ImageNet Roulette label

DeepDream, a software developed by Google in 2014, is a computer program designed to detect faces and other patterns in images. When the computer program is run in reverse, Google's DeepDream looks for faces everywhere. For example, when it is rendered through a convolutional neural network trained on ImageNet, Leonardo Da Vinci's *Mona Lisa* returns as the faces of dogs, frogs, and snakes. *Pareidolia*, the illusion of an image of something that does not exist (like the form of a face in a cloud), is more and more a technological concept.

The faces of Google's DeepDream are images beyond truth and falsehood, as much as they are beyond beautiful and ugly. The face is converted into a series of numerical values: for example, the position and relation between eyes, mouth, and nose, etcetera. There is no "shimmer of infinity,"[47] in contrast to the phenomenology of Emmanuel Levinas. There is no secret whatsoever behind the cheap smile of Google's *Mona Lisa*.

More and more, the only *shimmer* of the image is capital's. While the face is quantified and the smile is commodified, their surplus value is priced and valued by the industry of signs.[48]

As the duck face is replaced by the scrunch face, the faces of the users are used to generate more data for the images that they consume, like in a spin-off of *The Texas Chain Saw Massacre* set in the digital interface. Profile pictures on social media like Facebook are used by tech companies to train facial-recognition algrithms.[49]

47 Emmanuel Levinas, *Totality and Infinity*, tr. Alphonso Lingis, The Hague - Boston - London: Martinus Nijhoff, 1979, p. 207.

48 Geert Lovink, Narcissus Confirmed: Technologies of the Minimal Selfie, in Katharina Motyl and Regina Schober (eds) *The Failed Individual: Amid Exclusion, Resistance, and the Pleasure of Non-Conformity* (pp. 347 - 356), Frankfurt - New York: 2017.

FIGURE 9. Google DeepDream's *Mona Lisa*

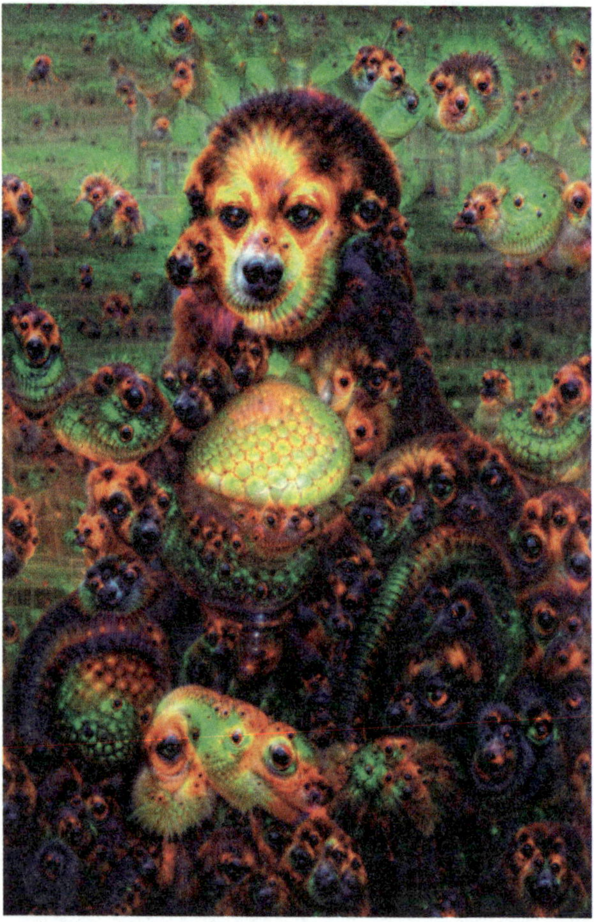

PAREIDOLIA
(/ˌpæɹ.aɪˈdəʊ.li.ə/)
the illusion of
an image of
something that
does not exist
IS MORE AND
MORE A TECH-
NOLOGICAL
CONCEPT

The body of the user is only a point of entry, like a fingertip, to the global network. The interface, as Byung-Chul Han writes about the face, is only a terminal to the system.[50] *Face detected*: your screen is unblocked. With the development of digital technology, hardware reverses into software and, now, to wetware. If Google's computer program looks for faces everywhere, it is because this is what Google does for capital: *keep its eyes on the consumer.*

The eye, as G. W. F. Hegel remarks in one of his lectures on fine art,[51] never meets another eye in the image. In principle, the sign of subjectivity is not reproducible as an image.
One day, it is said that Zeuxis painted a child with a bunch of grapes. Once again, the birds came to peck at the fruit. Then, the painter complained: "If only I had painted the child with verisimilitude, it would have scared the birds away!"[52]
According to Hegelian idealism, the light of the eye – the sign *par excellence* of the subject – cannot be reproduced by technical means. In this regard, eye-tracking technology is anti-Hegelian in principle. The end of eye-tracking technology is not only to capture the gaze but to look into its relation with the interface; it does not reproduce an image but rather ways of seeing as a part of user experience design (UXD). Therefore, the relation between the eye and the image is devalued.

49 Kashmir Hill, The Secretive Company That Might End Privacy as We Know It, *New York Times*, 18 January 2020, available at https://www.nytimes.com/2020/01/18/technology/clearview-privacy-facial-recognition.html.
50 Byung-Chul Han, *Saving Beauty*, tr. Daniel Steuer, Cambridge: Polity, 2018.
51 G. W. F. Hegel, *Aesthetics: Lectures on Fine Art*, Volume 1, tr. T. M. Knox, Oxford: Oxford University Press, 1975.
52 Pliny the Elder, *Natural History*, Book XXXV.

As a design tool, “eye tracking identifies and helps in the elimination of anything deemed confusing. These would be design elements endowed with some degree of ambiguity, indistinctness, unintelligibility, or other quality that would frustrate an immediate or effortless perceptual grasp,” as the art critic Jonathan Crary writes. “Eye tracking would detect a hesitancy, a kind of ‘stammering’ of eye movement that, even relatively briefly, is unable to settle into a secure fixation. But such minor sources of visual uncertainty and vagueness are corrected or removed in order to optimize ‘usability.’ ” [53]

As more and more eye-catching images are reproduced, there is less and less to see. There are no sights: there are views; the image is only another format of consumption. Therefore, there is no distinction between the light of the eye and the light of the image any longer. Thus, UXD does away with all shades and shadows, in the name of what is immediately visible and ready for consumption.

Are you still watching?

After a certain threshold, the high definition of the image is such that the latter returns as the optical illusion of the medium that reproduces it.

When Sagittarius A*, the black hole at the center of the Milky Way, is reproduced as an image by the Event Horizon Telescope, it is more than just a theory to the eyes of the viewers. In fact, it is no longer a matter of “belief” in one’s eyes but, instead, in the medium that reproduces them.

Yet, like in the Platonic allegory of the cave, [54] the image of Sagittarius A* does not depict the black hole

53 Jonathan Crary, *Scorched Earth: Beyond the Digital Age to a Post-Capitalist World*, London - New York: Verso, 2022, p. 83.

FIGURE 10. The first image of Sagittarius A*, the supermassive black hole at the center of the Milky Way

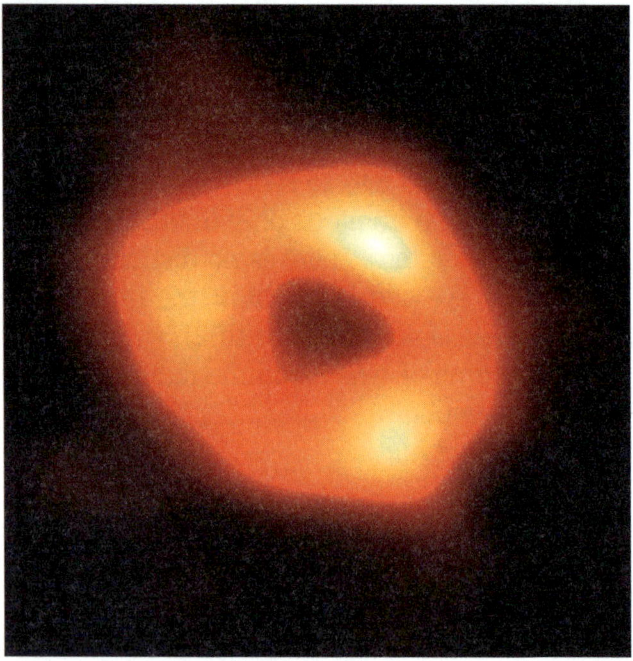

"The masses function as a gigantic black hole which inexorably inflects, bends and distorts all energy and light radiation approaching it."[55]

— Jean Baudrillard

55 Jean Baudrillard, *In the Shadow of the Silent Majorities or, The End of the Social and Other Essays*, p. 9.

itself but just its shadow: the event horizon does not emit light. In contrast with a first-order image of the black hole, the image of the Event Horizon Telescope reproduces only a way of seeing its magnetic field through the equations of general relativity. Again, the image is neither true nor false but only correct or incorrect according to its model.
In parallel with Sagittarius A*, the black hole in Christopher Nolan's *Interstellar* is a second-order image that was theorized according to the laws of physics as much as the laws of the economy. While the Event Horizon Telescope is unable to represent the singularity of the black hole, it was still able to render its radio interferometer data just in time for its re-release on IMAX. In the end, that "little maneuver" (as the protagonist of *Interstellar* says while the spacecraft leaves the black hole) cost only ten years, while it paid an extra $25 million at the box office.

After the linear perspective of the Renaissance, the axonometric perspective of capitalism is taken over by satellites, aerostats, and drones. In the twenty-first century, these technologies and their imagery reproduce the illusion of an all-seeing eye.[56]
Jon Rafman's *The Nine Eyes of Google Street View* is a photo project in which the artist shows the images of a world watched over by Google's machines. In one of the hundred screenshots taken from Street View - the software that puts together billions of images as a representation of the routes on Maps -, a group of four

54 Plato, Republic, tr. Paul Shorey, in Edith Hamilton and Huntington Cairns (eds) *The Collected Dialogues of Plato: Including the Letters* (pp. 575 - 844), Princeton: Princeton University Press, 1973.

56 For a similar argument, Hito Steyerl, *The Wretched of the Screen*, London: Sternberg Press, 2012.

men wait outside a house on fire in Atlanta. In another one, a woman gives the middle finger to the Google car driver and its camera. The nine-eyed camera not only reproduces the point of view of an all-seeing eye but also its indifferent stare. In contrast with the linear perspective of the Renaissance and Baroque, there is no moral dimension to the image.
When these images are used for self-driving car systems they are only operative images: they do not represent anything but only reproduce a sign for another machine.[57]

The logical paradox of evil is replaced by Google's corporate philosophy, whose slogan is "Don't be evil." It is not an answer to the question asked by theologians like Saint Augustine. As media theorist Ian Bogost writes in an article about the tech company: "For today's Google, evil isn't tied to malevolence or moral corruption, the customary senses of the term. Rather, it's better to understand Google's sense of evil as the disruption of its brand of (computational) progress." [58]
Google's evil is only *an engineering problem.*
The images of Google Maps and Google Street do *not* establish a new reality. They only take over the desert left over by its formalization.

In 1971, the United States abolished the conversion between the dollar and gold. The same year, the first personal computer, the Kenbak-1, was released, followed by the Altair 8800 in 1974. The first digital

57 For the concept of *operative image*, Harun Farocki (dir.), *Eye/Machine (I - III)*, Harun Farocki Filmproduktion, 2001 - 2003.

58 Ian Bogost, What Is "Evil" to Google?, 15 October 2013, *The Atlantic*, available at https://www.theatlantic.com/technology/archive/2013/10/what-is-evil-to-google/280573/.

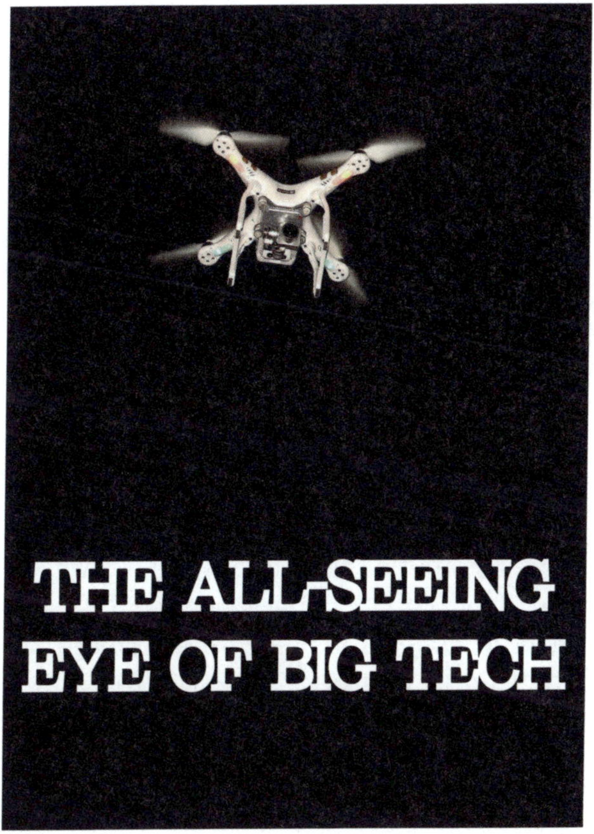

FIGURE 11. Drone.

technology designed for private use was sold in an economic system in which value was not based on the value of a metal but only on the market supply and demand.
It is the starting point of what Franco "Bifo" Berardi refers to as *semio-capitalism*.[59] The value of goods, which now includes semiotic ones like information, is no longer fixed. When digital technology takes the place of analog technology, the economy of images is more and more only a general economy of signs beyond beautiful and ugly, beyond truth and lie, beyond good and evil. There is no gold standard for the image anymore.
In 1975, Bill Gates and Paul Allen founded Microsoft to develop and sell software for the Altair 8800. Microsoft's mission statement was "a computer on every desk and in every home," but whose last part is: "*running Microsoft software*" (just like the fourth word of the French Revolution's motto is dropped after the Reign of Terror: "Liberty, Equality, Fraternity, or *Death*.")
The virtual image is only one more market of the capitalist economy.

Twenty minutes before digital technology there was Max Headroom, the first computer-generated TV host. *Max Headroom: 20 Minutes into the Future* is a cyberpunk television film in which society is controlled by the television conglomerate Zik-Zak and its subsidiary Network 23, hosted by computer-generated imagery of Max Headroom. The movie was a commercial success and the avatar of Max Headroom, played by actor Matt Frewer, debuted in his own show. The first episode of *The Max Headroom Show* was "Blipverts," in which

59 Franco "Bifo" Berardi, *The Uprising: On Poetry and Finance*, Los Angeles: Semiotext(e), 2012.

"SEMIO-CAPITALISM HAS TAKEN THE PLACE OF INDUSTRIAL CAPITALISM" [60] — "Bifo"

60 Franco "Bifo" Berardi, *And: Phenomenology of the End. Cognition and Sensibility in the Transition from Conjunctive to Connective Mode of Social Communication*, Helsinki: Aalto ARTS Books, 2014, p. 165.

FIGURE 12. Altair 8800 advertisement

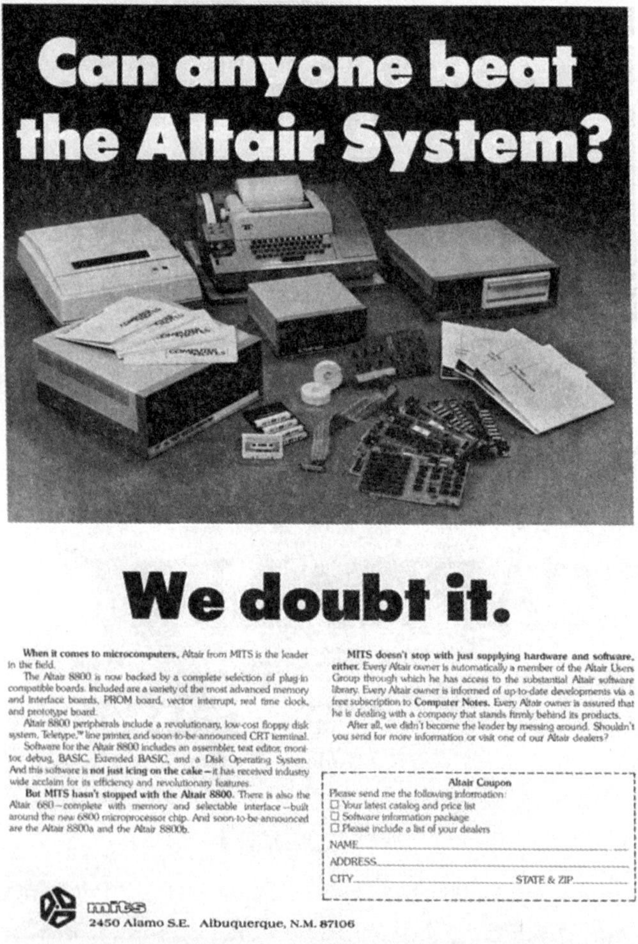

hyper-fast advertisements are used to capture the viewers' gaze in only a few seconds. But there is a side effect: the head of some viewers explodes due to the rate at which images are reproduced. The blipvert was for TV what, today, *content sludge* is for TikTok. "T-t-t-tune into Network 23! The network that's a *real* mind-blower!" [61] says Max Headroom - then, *boom!* His head explodes only to re-appear one second later. Produced in the twentieth century but set in the twenty-first, Network 23 broadcasts nothing but *brain rot.* Max Headroom was trash before trash. Before so-called virtual influencers like Lil Miquela (@lilmiquela), Shudu (@shudu.gram), and Aitana López (@fit_aitana), there was him, *the first computer-generated TV host.* He was the avatar of the near future.
Those who live by trash, only die by trash. On November 22nd, 1987, two television broadcasts were hijacked by an anonymous man, draped in a Max Headroom mask. For a minute and a half, the relation between the eye and the image is reproduced as such. The garble of the hijacker returns the trash of the image back to the medium. "I just made a giant masterpiece for the greatest world newspaper nerds!" After ninety seconds, the screen blacks out and the TV programming resumes.

61 Farhad Mann (dir.), *Max Headroom*, Season 1, Episode 1, 1987.

WE WILL BE RETURNING SHORTLY...

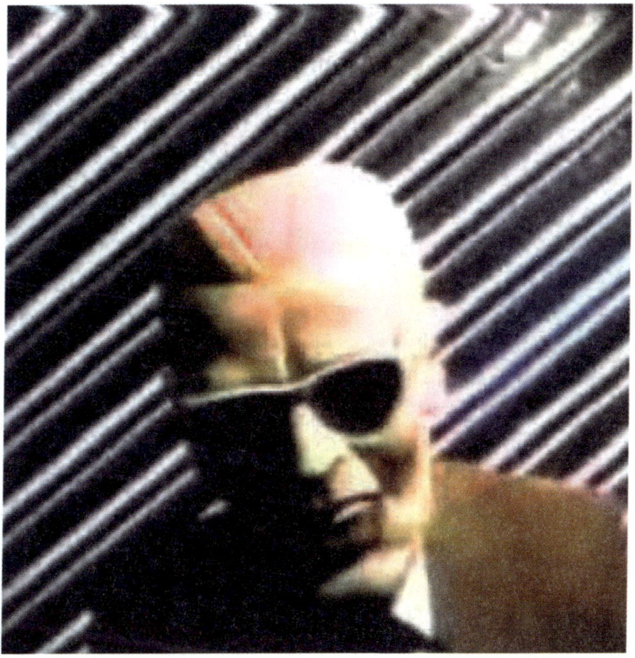

FIGURE 13. Max Headroom signal hijacking

Dear viewers,

THANK YOU FOR YOUR PATIENCE

In ancient times, those who believed in the representation of the image set out to destroy the simulacra. If there was something that escaped their fury, it was *less* real than reality: the representation of devils and demons. To return them to nothingness would mean too much; it would suppose that they were real in the first place. Today, on the other hand, the images are generally left untarnished. It is the reality behind them that is trashed. The reproduction of the images themselves already effaces it. In this regard, the Max Headroom hijacking did not show reality but only the dark glow of its abnegation.

If, according to an online theory, *the layout of printed circuit boards looks like demon sigils*, it is because we are still fascinated by the absence of meaning that occultism and esotericism left behind. "Boy I love trapping demons in microscopic silicon megastructures to do my bidding," a user nicknamed Lunar Princess Strife (@Strife212) tweeted in 2020, "I sure hope nothing goes wrong." [62]
The revival of the occult in the twenty-first century, from witchcraft to meme magick, is also a reaction to the cultural crisis of the image: the screen is the brand-new scrying mirror. When it is pushed to its limit, digital technology reverses into a medium to the otherworld.
To destroy your enemies, destroy their images. This is the first principle of magic of *The Golden Bough*. From a law of similarity, "the magician infers that he

[62] Lunar Princess Strife (@Strife212), AI = Applied Demonology, *X [Twitter]*, 30 April 2020, available at https://x.com/Strife212/status/1255789106522656773.

can produce any effect he desires merely by imitating it."[63] It is only as a postulate of this law that TikTok users believe that, insofar as two pictures are similar (like the printed circuit board and the demon sigil), their reality is the same. Like Solomon used the seal to control demons and force them to build his temple, the Internet influences its users and compels them to consume more.

In the end, the image is not destroyed but reproduced over and over. The ultimate act is deferred once again. Meanwhile, the "evil genius" of the image - capitalism - reproduces more and more of its signs.

Into the bargain, Pepe the Frog has been compared with the ancient Egyptian deity Kek, spelled also as Kuk. The androgynous god of darkness (or, rather, "dankness" as a 4chan user put it),[64] whose male form is depicted as a frog or a frog-headed man, has ever since been associated with the alt-right movement and Donald Trump. There is again only magic of the last order, which conjures its tricks with the magic spell of the medium.

"The future belongs to ghosts," Jacques Derrida says in the film *Ghost Dance*, directed by Ken McMullen. "The modern technology of images like cinematography and telecommunication enhances the power of ghosts and their ability to return to haunt us. In fact, it is because I wished to tempt the ghosts out that I agreed to

63 Sir James George Frazer, *The Golden Bough: A Study in Magic and Religion*, New York City: The Macmillan Company, 1925, p. 11.

64 Anonymous, What Can You Tell Me About Kuk, *4chan*, 27 November 2015, available at https://4archive.org/board/his/thread/312310.

FIGURE 14.
Seal of Solomon -
FIGURE 15.
PCB layout

14

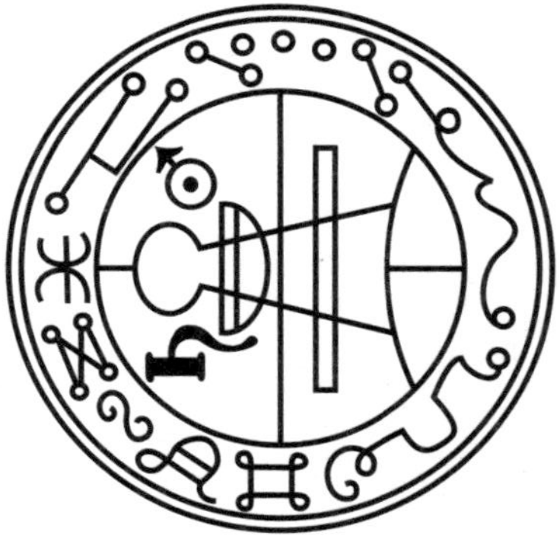

15

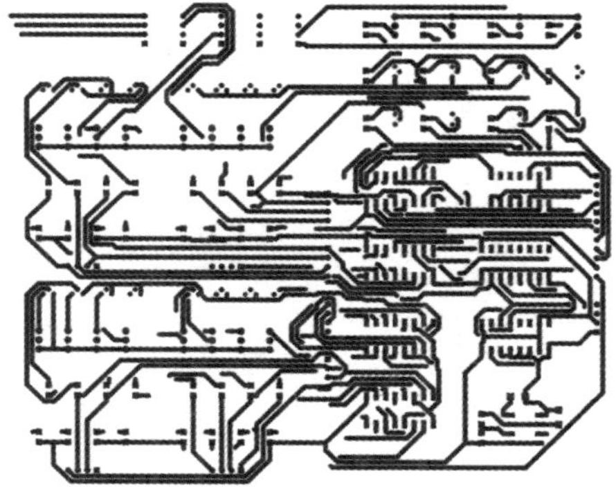

appear in this film." [65]

The ghost is not only the sign of the double. It is also the sign of the self-same. The ghost is the image of trash *par excellence*. The first picture of Samuel Beckett and King Bowser, in this regard, is phantasmatic not only because Samuel Beckett is dead (and King Bowser does not exist), but because it exists only as the repetition of that which has *not been as such*: yet another image. The ghost is none other than its ghostlore.

In Plato's doctrine, the *phantasma*-translated into Latin as *simulacrum*-is an image that appears to be more than an appearance. For instance, the veil of Parrhasius is a phantasm to Zeuxis, who is unable to see that it is an image. Yet, the fault of Zeuxis is not to believe the representation of the veil but that, when it is withdrawn, the truth remains truth; the fault of Zeuxis is imagination.

On the other hand, the artist of the *phantasma* is like any picture merchant, who exchanges one image for another. The phantasmagoria is always *the next image*. Hence, virtuality is displaced by virality. Whatever you see next is whatever you see now. In this regard, the spectacle is not only a series of images but the world-view that is materialized by means of it.

Capitalism is a story of ghosts in which everything is reproduced as an image and does not finish to return as such. Behind the image of Parrhasius, there is yet another veil.

65 Jacques Derrida in Ken McMullen (dir.), G*host Dance*, Channel Four, 1983 (my translation).

Nihilism is trending. The trend is, in Germanic languages, that which turns, runs, revolves, or bends in a certain direction, for example, a stream. Today, the medium is flowing relentlessly towards its conclusion: "restlessly, violently, headlong, like a river that wants to reach the end, that no longer reflects." [66] The *streaming* of the image does not reflect any sunlight anymore. The differences between true and false, beautiful and ugly, good and evil, are washed away. There are no more sights but only views.

We no longer believe in the great systems of value. The grand narrative of the image is finished. There is a new desert of the real.

This is the story of the end of the twenty-first century. "What I relate is the history of the next two centuries," Friedrich Nietzsche writes in 1887-1888. "I describe what is coming, what can no longer come differently: *the advent of nihilism*." [67] The whole history of civilization is a futile attempt to hide the fact that images do not represent anything whatsoever. They no longer have any meaning. They lack any values as such.

"For why has the advent of nihilism become *necessary*?" the German philosopher asks in his Preface to *The Will to Power*, published posthumously by his sister Elisabeth Förster-Nietzsche. "Because the values we have had hitherto thus draw their final consequence; because nihilism represents the ultimate logical conclusion of our great values and ideals - because we must experience nihilism before we can find out what value these 'values' really had. - We require, sometime, *new values*." [68]

Before the end of the century, there will be no more

[66] Friedrich Nietzsche, *The Will to Power*, p. 3.
[67] Friedrich Nietzsche, *The Will to Power*, p. 3.
[68] Friedrich Nietzsche, *The Will to Power*, p. 4.

FIGURE 16. Bliss Microsoft screensaver.

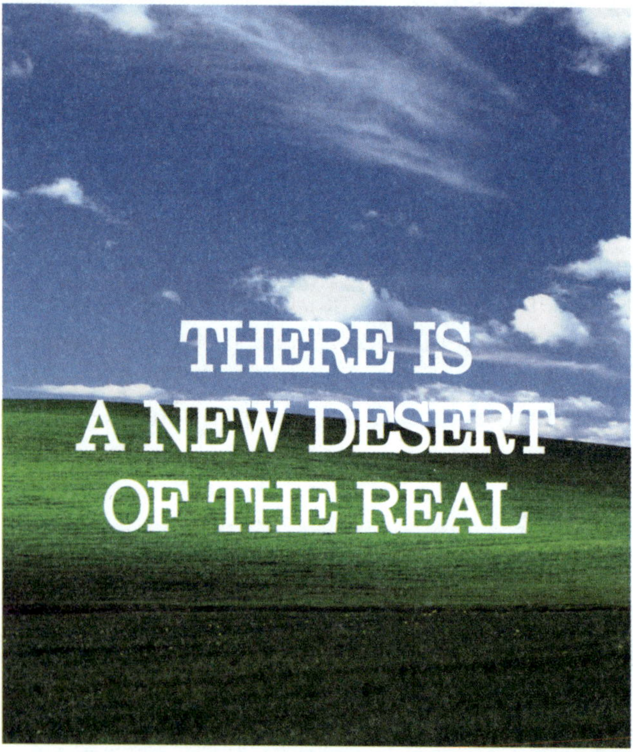

images as such. Rather than waiting and seeing, the medium of the image is going to be pushed beyond the limit. As he writes in his *Zarathustra*, "if something is falling, one should also give it a push! Everything of today - it is falling, it is failing: who would want to stop it!" [69]

Every medium, once it is pushed to its limit, reverses its characteristics.[70] Painting, beyond the trompe-l'œil, is inverted into the effacement of reality: it no longer competes with appearance but with the light of the eye as such. Earlier than the first photograph of Nicéphore Niépce, the image of the classical age already reproduced the eye for it. The same is at issue with the last stage of the image two centuries after the invention of photography.

It is not only when the picture is the most realistic, like Zeuxis's bunch of grapes, but when it does not have any relationship with reality that it is beyond all representation. The highest point of the image is also its lowest.

The image is reversed into its negative. It is no longer the mirror of reality. It is not the sign of that which *has been*, as Roland Barthes's photography,[71] but that which *has not been*; it is not the image of the past but the re-imagination of the present. Nothing is able to overcome the digital medium except the digital medium itself.

69 Friedrich Nietzsche, *Thus Spoke Zarathustra: A Book for All and None*, tr. Adrian del Caro, Cambridge: Cambridge University Press, 2006, p. 168.

70 For more, Marshall McLuhan and Bruce R. Powers, *The Global Village: Transformations in World Life and Media in the 21st Century*, New York - Oxford: Oxford University Press, 1989.

71 Roland Barthes, *Camera Lucida*, tr. Richard Howard, London: Vintage, 2000.

THE TWENTY-FIRST CENTURY WILL BE NIETZSCHEAN

The re-formatted medium is not only another technology but another relationship with it: new values. Its imagery is global, but it no longer "represents" global culture. *Take a good look!*

When the image is seen under the optics of the medium, it is no longer viewed at the level of locality but globality. Any new relation with it is also another relation in general with the medium, which is neither real nor virtual but both practical and theoretical.
As Yuk Hui's cosmotechnics joins the frame, the differences among the means of the image across the globe cannot be *unseen*[72] (even when it is a low-quality and highly-compressed JPEG file). Take another look at the radically different sense of humor of Chinese memes, like the Panda Head, referred to as *biaoqing*. The Mandarin word *biaoqing* may be translated into English as *emoticon*; however, in contrast with Western memetics (the Panda Head has been compared to the Wojak meme), the *biaoqing* is part of a vernacular of its own that makes references to the country's history and tradition, as well as the collective identity of Chinese netizens. While it is trashed at the level of the image (i.e., Eastern memes appear similar to Western memes), it is at the level of the medium that the Panda Head, which went viral on social media in 2023, junks the value of the sign that is represented in a *unilateral way* by the Occident. "Eat shit!" as the bottom text of one Panda Head *biaoqing* has it.
Like Friedrich Nietzsche sought the revaluation of Western-European values through the construction of a new way to Southern Europe (at a time in which the transalpine tunnels literally built them to the sound of

72 Yuk Hui, *Art and Cosmotechnics*, New York: e-flux, 2021.

FIGURE 17. Panda Head meme

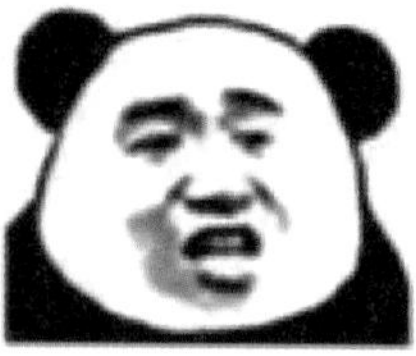

食屎啦你!
EAT SHIT!

dynamite),[73] the revaluation of the image is reproduced by means of the electronic superhighway.
As the eyes look further into the medium, they also start to be able to see beyond it. Instead of the West going towards the East and the East going towards the West, as Marshall McLuhan believed,[74] the re-formatted medium reproduces another pair of eyes that are able to look farther than its foreseeable end. A whole new world is in sight; its imagery is coming into view.

In the 2010s, theorists like Mark Fisher and Simon Reynolds noted an inability to imagine the future. In the 2020s, on the other hand, according to Grafton Tanner, "a startling trend had emerged, something far more disturbing: an inability to imagine the present." [75] But while the image of politics and culture are freeze-framed, only digital technology appears to move forward: from software updates and new generations of smartphones to the new spring of artificial intelligence.
As analog technology shifts to digital technology, value also shifts from temporal to spatial: the point of view is global.
In his video-essay *Sinofuturism (1839-2046 AD)*, Lawrence Lek argues that since "the physical

[73] Peter Sloterdijk, "I Am Not a Man, I Am Dynamite": Peter Sloterdijk on Nietzsche, *Los Angeles Review of Books*, 17 May 2018, available at https://lareviewofbooks.org/entitled-opinions/not-man-dynamite-peter-sloterdijk-nietzsche/.
[74] Marshall McLuhan, *Understanding Media: The Extensions of Man*, London - New York: Ark, 1987.
[75] Grafton Tanner, *The Hours Have Lost Their Clock: The Politics of Nostalgia*, London: Zer0 Books, 2021, p. 10. For more, Simon Reynolds, *Retromania: Pop Culture's Addiction to its Own Past*, London: Faber & Faber, 2010 and Mark Fisher, *Ghosts of My Life: Writings on Depression, Hauntology and Lost Futures*, London: Zer0 Books, 2014.

components of high technology are literally made in China, it makes no sense to produce visions of the future. It's already here."[76] If the reproduction of the image is more and more *with Chinese characteristics*, it is because the machinery used to make is produced in China. The future, as that which is the farthest, is also the nearest.

However, the value according to which the image is reproduced is always one and the same: capital. "Sinofuturism may replace Americanism in the near future, yet there is no opening to the future in this shift." [77] Indeed, in a system in which everything is reproduced as an image, even before it is imagined as such, there is no eye-opening to the *present*.

"Normal people can't imagine how these teenagers in our center use the Internet."[78] Today, imagination is equal to the faculty to envision another relation with the medium. Imagination is not an image but what is always after and against the technology of the image.

From the viewpoint of the economy, the image is nothing else than the sign of capital. In general, the capitalist system does not see anything but a blur in the place of the image, in which anyone is, by default, exchangeable with another (like gold with gold). The short-termism of the economy, critiqued in the twenty-first century by post-Marxist theorists as Bernard Stiegler,[79] is equivalent to the short-sightedness of the commodity form. Capitalism - whether in its Western or Eastern version - overfocuses only on what is produced

76 Lawrence Lek (dir.), *Sinofuturism (1839 - 2046 AD)*, available at https://sinofuturism.com/.

77 Yuk Hui, *Art and Cosmotechnics*, New York: e-flux, 2021, p.76.

78 Tao Ran (Director of Daxing Internet Addiction Treatment Center) in Lawrence Lek (dir.), *Sinofuturism (1839 - 2046 AD)*.

79 For example, Bernard Stiegler, *For a New Critique of Political Economy*, tr. Daniel Ross, Cambridge: Polity, 2010.

REPRODUCE
REPRODUCE
REPRODUCE
REPRODUCE
REPRODUCE...

more and more *immediately*: the sign of capital.
But as soon as the image is put into the focus of the economy, the latter loses sight of its first target: the subject. Whilst the economy takes priority over politics, the image is able to reproduce the eyes of another subjectivity that is no longer short-sighted. The efficient cause of technology replaces its final cause.
In fact, if the function of the image is short-termist, it is only insofar as the image reproduces itself without end that it is able to reproduce another subject. The short-sightedness of the image is reversed into the long-sightedness of the imaginary. The question is no longer to render another image but to envision another relationship with the medium as a whole.

For a long time, the power of the image was an index of its principle of representation. In fact, only insofar as an image stands in for something, it is able to capture it. *Smile, you are on camera!* However, the same science of the image that provides the latter with its tools (camera sensors, optical filters, signal processors, and so on) is the same one that reverts its logic from visibility to invisibility, from representation to its negation. As the science of the image progresses, it trashes itself.
Take a good look at the "invisibility cloak" designed by ISHU in 2016, which makes its wearer invisible to flash photography. Made with a blend of cotton and highly reflective materials, it is a blend of "fashion with technology" that "elevates your style but also protects your privacy [...], ensuring unwanted photos and videos are presented on platforms like Instagram and Snapchat." [80] ISHU's anti-paparazzi clothing has been

80 ISHU, Signature ISHU Scarf, 2016, available at https://theishu.com/products/the-ishu?variant=41949781655575.

FIGURES 18 - 19. Paris Hilton
wearing signature ISHU scarf

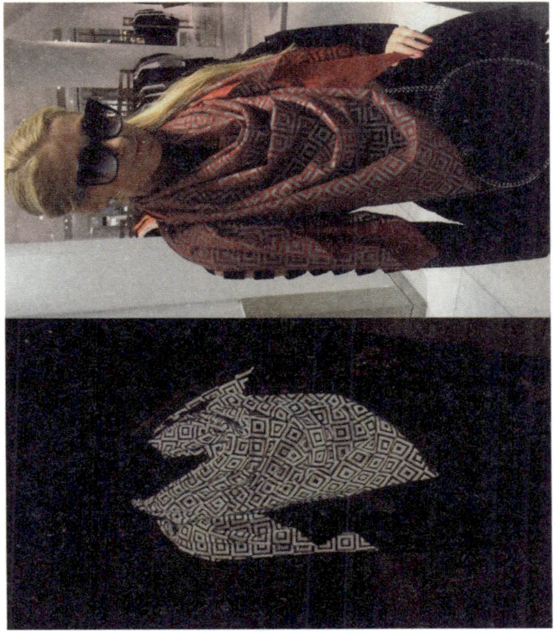

used by popular celebrities like Paris Hilton, who is featured in the product description above-cited, alongside Kevin Hart, Cameron Diaz, and Nick Jonas. The listing price is £1,550-1,650. It is currently available in three colours: black, red, and grey.
While science ranges against magic,[81] it is within science that another relation with the image takes place. Sight is no longer the noblest of the senses, as René Descartes writes in the first page of his essay on dioptrics,[82] but the *trashiest*.

Ever since its first experiments, the technology of the image has been tainted by a racist eyesight. As color photography developed, its science was based on the categorization of lighter skin tones as the norm (and darker skin tones as the abnormal). Since the target market of the image is that of lighter skin tones, the latter were the baseline of its technics. But when Kodak, the largest photography company of the time, received a series of complaints about the color of dark and milk chocolate, then, the technique to reproduce darker tones in Kodak's products, which included the skin color of black people, was upgraded.[83] You *consume* with your eyes first, as the Ancient Roman proverb has it. More and more, you consume with your eyes *only*.
The medium does not *produce* anything. It only reproduces the relation between the eye and the image. On the other hand, any tear in the hole of this relation opens the eyes to another relation with the medium itself.

81 For more, Vilém Flusser, *Towards a Philosophy of Photography*.
82 René Descartes, Optics.
83 Sarah Lewis, The Racial Bias Built Into Photography, *The New York Times*, 25 April 2019, available at https://www.nytimes.com/2019/04/25/lens/sarah-lewis-racial-bias-photography.html.

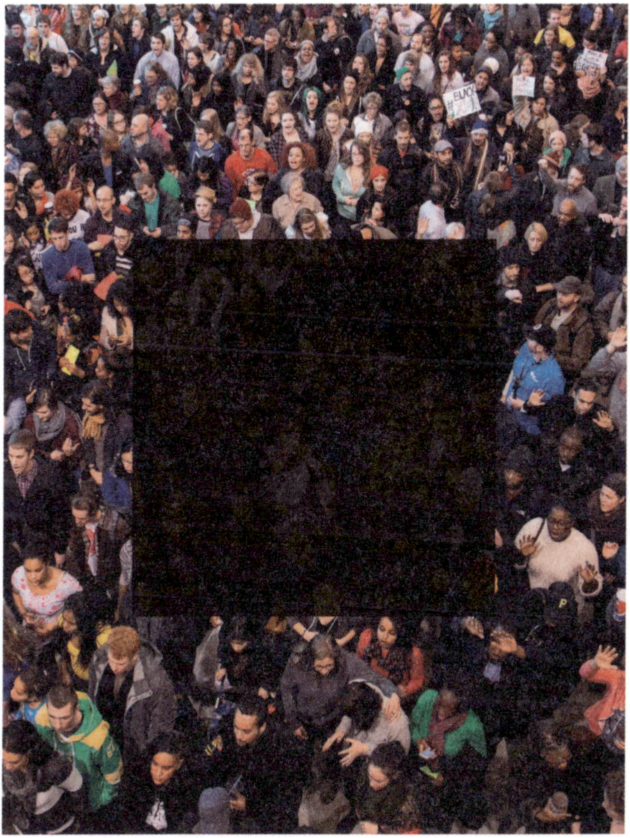

FIGURE 20. Black square on Black Lives Matter protest

On the first Tuesday of June 2020, millions of black squares were posted on social media following the death in police custody of George Floyd. In the context of the The Show Must Be Paused campaign, the posts pledged to disrupt business as usual in protest against racism. More than 28 million people posted a black picture with the hashtags #BlackoutTuesday and #BlackLivesMatter. Popular celebrities like Britney Spears, Katy Perry, and Kylie Jenner went dark on social media.
While George Floyd was arrested and murdered because he used a fake $20 bill in a convenience store, the black square reproduces another relationship between image and its consumption. One day prior to Blackout Tuesday, television networks including MTV, Paramount, Nickelodeon, and Comedy Central showed a black screen with the words "I can't breathe" for 8 minutes and 46 seconds, the time George Floyd was choked by the knee of police officer Derek Chauvin. For more than the blink of an eye, the relationship between the eye and the image is disrupted. The eyes do not stare into the screen but after and against it. Then, 8 minutes and 46 seconds later, the image of the spectacle is resumed; yet, another pair of eyes has already been reproduced *by means of it.*
The black square is not the sign of an anti-racist reality. It is, however, the sign of another medium in which the paradigm of visibility is reversed. On the one hand, the black square has been criticized as a form of slacktivism and political nihilism which disrupted Black Lives Matter hashtags and reproduced its politics into an aesthetic trend. On the other hand, when looked at without a short-sighted eye, the black square *did not reproduce at the level of the image but the medium.* There is nothing to see and, yet, there is an image. It

is the *foresight* of another relation with the medium.

If today, capitalism is based on an economy of images, the only strategy is against the value of images themselves. More and more, the images are reproduced *against* their own logic.
At the end of March 2023, Donald Trump was indicted by a court jury for his role in paying hush money to porn star Stormy Daniels. A few days before, several fake images were generated using artificial intelligence showing the arrest of the former president. In one picture, Donald Trump is grabbed by police officers. In another one, he is wearing an orange jumpsuit and brooming or mopping the jail's floor. Meanwhile, in another series of pictures, he is planning his escape through the sewers. Once he is out of jail, the ex-president goes to a McDonald's (misspelled as "Minonad") where, while he is still dressed in the prisoner's orange jumpsuit, which is now paired with a color-matching cap, he orders chicken nuggets and a Coke. Finally, he sits down at a yellow table and cries.
The series of deepfakes was created with Midjourney and prompted by journalist Eliot Higgins (@EliotHiggins) who posted them in a social media thread. The first caption reads: "Making pictures of Trump getting arrested while waiting for Trump's arrest."[84] Following the viral thread on X (formerly Twitter), he was banned from Midjourney and the word "arrest" was restricted from use in the generative artificial intelligence service. "Apparently doing a viral thread about Donald

[84] Eliot Higgins (@EliotHiggins), Making Pictures of Trump Getting Arrested while Waiting for Trump's Arrest, *Twitter [X]*, 20 March 2023, available at https://x.com/EliotHiggins/status/1637927681734987777.

FIGURE 21.
Trump's arrest

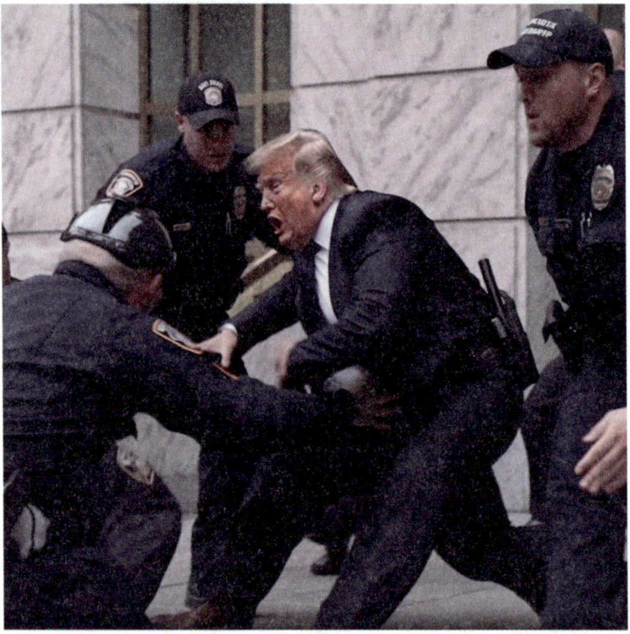

"With the true world, we have also abolished the apparent one!"[85]

— Friedrich Nietzsche

[85] Friedrich Nietzsche, Twilight of the Idols, in Walter Kaufmann, *The Portable Nietzsche* (pp. 463 - 564), tr. Walter Kaufmann, Middlesex: Penguin Books, 1984, p. 486.

Trump using Midjourney images is enough to get you banned from Midjourney, oops."[86]
Once again, these images are not the sign of an anti-capitalist reality. Although Donald Trump was the first president to be found guilty of thirty-four felony convictions, it did not prevent America's most famous businessman from being re-elected president of the United States the following year.

"Meanwhile in AI Trump world" is the caption of one picture that has been viewed over half a million times.[87] But the image is no longer believed to represent the relation between *this* and *another* world: there is nothing behind the curtain. When the true world is abolished, as Friedrich Nietzsche remarked, there is no longer any apparent world.[88]
The image is not *about* Donald Trump anymore. The difference between reality and *virality* is trashed. The image no longer casts any shadow, to put it in Nietzschean terms. If the image of Donald Trump is stained, it is because Donald Trump is *nothing* beyond the medium of the image ("cosmetics has replaced ideology,"[89] as an American media theorist once wrote). Those who live by trash, only die by trash...

In May 2024, the AI-generated image of a refugee camp in the desert went viral on Instagram. Hundreds and hundreds of tents are depicted in a God's-eye view. In the middle of the image, the whiter tents are

86 Eliot Higgins (@EliotHiggins), Apparently Doing a Viral Thread about Donald Trump Using Midjourney, *Twitter [X]*, 22 March 2023, available at https://x.com/EliotHiggins/status/1638470303310389248.
87 Eliot Higgins (@EliotHiggins), Meanwhile, in AI Trump World, *Twitter [X]*, 21 March 2023, available at https://x.com/EliotHiggins/status/1638114034263240704.
88 Friedrich Nietzsche, Twilight of the Idols.
89 Neil Postman, *Amusing Ourselves to Death: Public Discourse in the Age of Show Business*, York: Metheun, 1987.

arranged to spell out the words "ALL EYES ON RAFAH." Two months before the viral post by Amirul Shah (@shahv4012), the phrase was stated by Richard Peeperkorn, the Director of WHO's Office of the Occupied Palestinian Territories, following the announcement by the Israel government of an upcoming ground operation on Rafah, the southernmost city in the Gaza Strip.

In contrast with other images of Israel's war, which are restricted due to graphic content ("To protect users from disturbing imagery…"),[90] the AI-generated image of Rafah was *liked* and shared 50 million times across social media from all over the world, including popular celebrities: from Kid Cudi to Gigi and Bella Hadid.

If the image was reproduced in the social media feed, while many other images of the Israel-Palestinian conflict did not (and still do not), it is because it trashed the principle of representation.

All eyes are *not* on Rafah: they are only staring at the screen. Nevertheless, this is where the so-called war of images takes place. Meta, which owns and operates Instagram and Facebook, is complicit in the censorship of pro-Palestinian images,[91] from the moderation of posts with the term "Zionist" to the shadow-banning of pro-Palestinian users. The policy of colonialism is only pursued *by other media*, to update the Prussian general's famous dictum.[92]

Even if *All Eyes on Rafah* does not represent the back-

[90] Meta, Violent and Graphic Content, *Transparency Center*, available at https://transparency.meta.com/en-gb/policies/community-standards/violent-graphic-content/.

[91] Kelly Lewis, Social Media Platforms Are Complicit in Censoring Palestinian Voices, *The Conversation*, 24 May 2021, available at https://theconversation.com/social-media-platforms-are-complicit-in-censoring-palestinian-voices-161094.

[92] Carl von Clausewitz, *On War*, tr. Michael Howard and Peter Paret, Oxford: Oxford University Press, 2007

FIGURE 23.
Watermelon logo

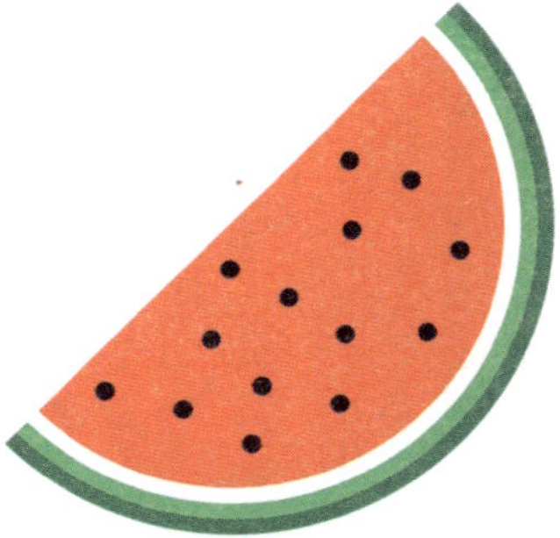

FIGURE 22.
All Eyes on Rafah

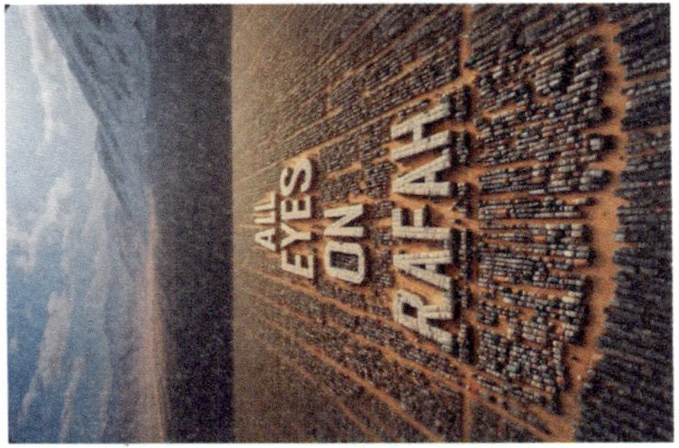

ground of the military operation, it foregrounds the mediatic operation itself. The image has no relation to the city of Rafah: the latter is only a junkyard for the bombs and the trash around them. At the same time, it is theorized in contrast with the medium as such by tearing a hole in the curtain of colonialism.
The image is not the sign of a decolonized reality. It is, nevertheless, the sign of an anti-colonialist medium. More than 50 million times, the global eyes move away from the colonialist medium to an anti-colonialist one. *Warning: this post contains trash which some media companies may find disturbing.* The virtual earth, on which the global eyes laid upon since October 7th, 2023, is scorched.
There is another desert where before there was only junk.

It is not possible to evaluate the image according to the oldest of values: representation. For hundreds of years, the value of the image was nothing more than a *theoretical* problem. But in the last stage of the image, it is reproduced more and more before the very eyes of the viewers. In fact, it is the eyes of the viewers that now behold the value of the image. In other words, value is no longer a matter of theory but praxis; it is not qualitative but quantitative.
As a sign, the image is used in order to reproduce more capital, without regard to whether the trend is capitalist or anti-capitalist, racist or anti-racist, colonialist or anti-colonialist. According to the logic of trash: the image is trashy because it is global; it is global because it is trashy. Then, *the same logic trashes* twenty-five centuries of metaphysics (or twenty-four, depending on which theoretician you ask).
The more the image is reproduced, the more valuable

it is. But the more the value of the image is equivalent only to its reproduction in the economy of signs, the more its value is trashed: it no longer refers to anything else other than the reproduction of capital. The disvaluation of the image is both the cause and the effect of the political economy of signs. Rather than representation, its principle is reproduction.
The devaluation of the image is only the beginning of its revalorization and revolution. Today, the function of the image is no longer in the background but in the foreground (video monetization and image tokenization, too, are only another visual content in the stream). Then, the function of the image is reproduced before the very eyes of the viewers; the image format is converted to imagination as it is no longer possible to avert one's gaze from the medium and its mode of reproduction. If the final cause is only the reproduction of the eyes of the viewers, the reversal of the medium pushes it beyond its own end.

What happens when Jean Baudrillard's *Simulacra and Simulation* is a bestseller on Amazon.com? In the twenty-first century, the scale of the simulation is not local but global. The simulation is a trend.
On the one hand, there is the simulation theory of *The Matrix*, according to which reality is nothing more than a computer-generated image made by machines who have enslaved humanity for their own reproduction. Nevertheless, it is possible to distinguish between the blue pill and the red pill and make a choice between Matrix and Zion, between the inside and the outside of Plato's cave. "No one can be told what the Matrix is. You have to see it for yourself. This is your last chance. After this, there is no turning back. You take the blue pil-the story ends, you wake up in your

WHAT HAPPENS WHEN JEAN BAUDRILLARD'S *SIMULACRA AND SIMULATION* IS A BESTSELLER ON AMAZON.COM?

bed and believe whatever you want to believe. You take the red pill-you stay in Wonderland, and I show you how deep the rabbit hole goes."[93]

On the other hand, there is the simulation theory of Jean Baudrillard's *Simulacra and Simulation*, which was the model for *The Matrix* and has been a required reading for the actors in the films directed by the Wachowskis. In an interview following the release of the third title in the franchise, Jean Baudillard stated, ironically, that this "is surely the kind of film about the matrix that the matrix would have been able to produce,"[94] or *reproduce*. In fact, the message of *The Matrix* franchise is equal to its own reproduction on a global scale by means of the proliferation of its signages. As the relation between the image of *The Matrix* and its reproduction is more and more graphic, the simulation does not uphold the values of representation anymore. Reproduction takes precedence over production. The imagery is no longer watched for what it represents but how it reproduces itself; the masses no longer look out for the curtain to ring down but for the *encore*. "I am sure you can understand why our beloved parent company, Warner Bros., has decided to make a sequel to the trilogy"[95] (Agent Smith in *The Matrix Resurrections*). But as they see through the image and into its reproduction, they also start to imagine another relationship with the medium.

It is the masses that remake the simulation. In this

93 The Wachowskis (dir.), *The Matrix*, Warner Bros., Village Roadshow Pictures, 1999.

94 Jean Baudrillard, The Matrix Decoded: Interview with Aude Lancelin (AL), tr. Gary Genosko and Adam Bryx, in Richard G. Smith and David B. Clarke (eds.), *From Hyperreality to Disappearance: The Uncollected Interviews* (pp. 179 - 181), Edinburgh: Edinburgh University Press, 2015, p. 180.

95 The Wachowskis (dir.), *The Matrix Resurrections*, Warner Bros., Village Roadshow Pictures, 2021.

regard, there is no dichotomy between the simulation of *The Matrix* franchise and the one repeated by Baudrillardian theory. The only disparity is the relation between the eye and the image as such.

If it is easier to imagine the end of the world than the end of trash, it is because *trash is the end of the world.* Two centuries after the technological revolution, the image of the end of the world and the medium are not distinguishable from each other anymore. The same year Elon Musk was announced Time's Person of the Year, the image of an old Greek woman crying amid a wildfire in Greece was on the cover of the same magazine's best photographs of 2021. The difference between capitalism and the end of the world is effaced.

Again and again, the end of the world is the *hottest* trend right now. Take a look at the image of the Hollywood sign on fire created with Grok, Elon Musk's chatbot, that went viral on social media during the wildfires in the region. Before the end of the twenty-first century, wildfires like the ones that scorched the earth near the Hollywood Sign will multiply due to the acceleration of climate change; meanwhile, the quantity of images is going to increase in a similar way according to the corollary of Moore's law.

Although there are no words left to describe the end of the world, there is always another image and a sad emoji ready to substitute them. The difference between the spectacular image of the Hollywood fires and less spectacular ones is none insofar as both reproduce the same number of signs. In the third millennium, there is no return to true and false appearances: the reproduction of the end has superseded its representation.

When the last picture is posted on social media, there will still be at least one computer program to *like* and share it... To paraphrase Walter Benjamin, the catastrophe *is* that the reproduction of capitalism just goes on and on.[96] The question concerning technology

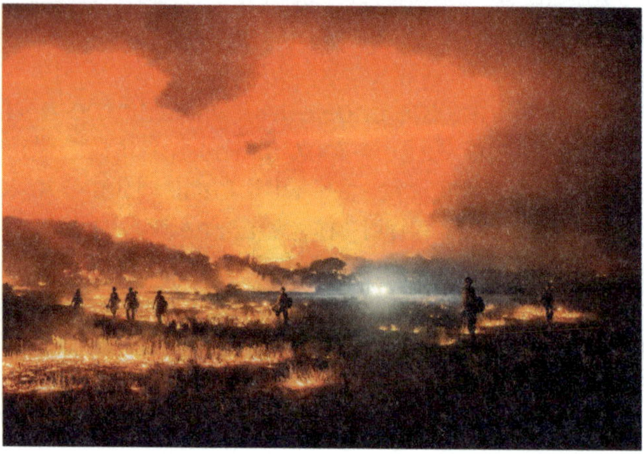

FIGURE 24. Pine Gulch fire

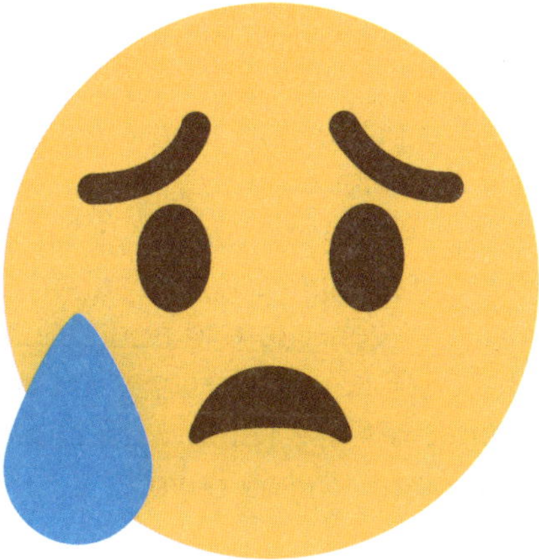

FIGURE 25. Sad emoji

in the twenty-first century is also about the *final* cause of capital (spoiler: it is more capital).
The ghost of extinction is now available in streaming. If "social media are designed for doomscrolling,"[97] as Geert Lovink argues in his essay *Extinction Internet*, it is not merely because "bad vibes" reproduce twice as much engagement as "good" ones, but because the *ultimate logical conclusion* of the medium is no longer different from the end of the world as such. The image of the end and the end of the image are one and the same.
When Just Stop Oil protesters threw tomato soup over the artworks of Western culture, the two paintings by Vincent Van Gogh were untarnished: the images were exhibited behind a transparent screen; instead, it was the relationship between the eye and the image that was blemished. What is worth *more*, art or the end of the world? As the eyes are filled with the glow of the screen, they also begin to see beyond it.

The value of the image is no longer *overestimated*. Its format is not transcendental: it is immanent. Its logic is not linear and irreversible: it is circular and reversible. Its principle is not representation: it is reproduction. It is not a mirror of reality: it is a screen to capitalism.
The image does not reflect any sunlight anymore. "What were we doing when we unchained this earth from its sun? Whither is it moving now? Whither are we moving? Away from all suns? Are we not

96 Walter Benjamin, *The Arcades Project*, tr. Howard Eiland and Kevin McLaughlin, Cambridge: Belknap Press, 1999.
97 Geert Lovink, *Extinction Internet: Our Inconvenient Moment of Truth*, Amsterdam: Institute of Network Cultures, 2022, p. 33.

plunging continually? Backward, sideward, forward, in all directions? Is there still any up or down? Are we not straying as through an infinite nothing? Do we not feel the breath of empty space? Has it not become colder? Is not night continually closing in on us? Do we not need to light lanterns in the morning?"[98]

[98] Friedrich Nietzsche, *Gay Science*, p. 181.

FIGURE 26. Broken picture

Reference list

Angelicism01. Heidegger on NFTs: A 'Translation' by Angelicism01 RIP. From The Turning, *Substack*, 4 March 2021, https://ia800603.us.archive.org/35/items/angelicism01-email-archive/20210403-HEIDEGGER%20ON%20NFTS-221.txt.

Anonymous. What Can You Tell Me About Kuk, *4chan*, 27 November 2015, https://4archive.org/board/his/thread/312310.

Barthes, Roland. *Camera Lucida*, tr. Richard Howard, London: Vintage, 2000.

Baudrillard, Jean. *Simulacra and Simulation*, tr. Sheila Faria Glaser, Ann Arbor: University Of Michigan Press, 1981.

_____. *In the Shadow of the Silent Majorities or, The End of the Social and Other Essays*, tr. Paul Foss, Paul Patton, and John Johnston, Los Angeles: Semiotext(e), 1983.

_____. *Symbolic Exchange and Death*, tr. Iain Hamilton Grant, London, Thousand Oaks, New Delhi: SAGE Publications, 1993.

_____. The Matrix Decoded: Interview with Aude Lancelin (AL), tr. Gary Genosko and Adam Bryx, in Richard G. Smith and David B. Clarke (eds.), *From Hyperreality to Disappearance: The Uncollected Interviews* (pp. 179 - 181), Edinburgh: Edinburgh University Press, 2015.

Benjamin, Walter. *The Arcades Project*, tr. Howard Eiland and Kevin McLaughlin, Cambridge: Belknap Press, 1999.

_____. *The Work of Art in the Age of Mechanical Reproduction*, tr. J. A. Underwood, London: Penguin, 2008.

Berardi, Franco"Bifo". *The Uprising: On Poetry and Finance*, Los Angeles: Semiotext(e), 2012.

_____. *And: Phenomenology of the End. Cognition and Sensibility in the Transition from Conjunctive to Connective Mode of Social Communication*, Helsinki: Aalto ARTS Books, 2014.

Bogost, Ian. What Is "Evil" to Google?, 15 October 2013, *The Atlantic*, https://www.theatlantic.com/technology/archive/2013/10/what-is-evil-to-google/280573/.

Borges, Jorge Luis. *The Book of Sand*, tr. Norman Thomas di Giovanni, New York: E. P. Dutton, 1977.

Bridle, James. The Nightmare Videos of Childrens' YouTube — and What's Wrong with the Internet Today, April 2018, *Ted*, https://www.ted.com/talks/james_bridle_the_nightmare_videos_of_children_s_youtube_and_what_s_wrong_with_the_internet_today/reading-list.

_____. *New Dark Age: Technology and the Future*, London - Brooklyn: Verso, 2018.

Bright, Kevin S. (dir.). *Friends*, Season 9, Episode 23, NBC, 2003.

BuzzFeed (@BuzzFeed). @KimKardashian Apparently It's Black and Blue, *X [Twitter]*, 27 February 2015, https://x.com/BuzzFeed/status/571168834092199936.

Conti, Adolfo (dir.). *Plakat: The Birth of Modern Advertising*, ARTE, 2018.

Crary, Jonathan. *Scorched Earth: Beyond the Digital Age to a Post-Capitalist World*, London - New York: Verso, 2022.

Crawford, Kate. *Atlas of AI: Power, Politics, and the Planetary Costs of Artificial Intelligence*, New Haven - London: Yale University Press, 2021.

Crawford, Kate and Paglen, Trevor. *ImageNet Roulette* [Artwork], 2019.

_____. Excavating AI: The Politics of Images in Machine Learning Training Sets, *Excavating AI*, 19 September 2019, https://excavating.ai/.

Dante. *The New Life*, tr. Dante Gabriel Rossetti, London: Ellis and Elvey, 1899.

Derrida, Jacques. *Writing and Difference*, tr. Alan Bass, Chicago: University of

Chicago Press, 1978.
Descartes, René. Optics, in *Discourse on Method, Optics, Geometry, and Meteorology* (pp. 65 - 176), tr. Paul J. Olscamp, Indianapolis - Cambridge: Hackett, 2001.
Duchamp, Marcel. *L.H.O.O.Q.* [Artwork], The Carl Fredrik Reuterswärd Art Foundation, 1919.
Farocki, Harun (dir.). *Eye/Machine (I - III)*, Harun Farocki Filmproduktion, 2001 - 2003.
Federici, Silvia. *Revolution at Point Zero: Housework, Reproduction, and Feminist Struggle*, Oakland: PM Press, 2012.
Fisher, Mark. *Ghosts of My Life: Writings on Depression, Hauntology and Lost Futures*, London: Zer0 Books, 2014.
Flusser, Vilém. *Towards a Philosophy of Photography*, tr. Anthony Mathews, London: Reaktion, 2006.
Frazer, James George. *The Golden Bough: A Study in Magic and Religion*, New York City: The Macmillan Company, 1925.
Gerritzen, Mieke and Lovink, Geert. *Made in China, Designed in California, Criticised in Europe: Amsterdam Design Manifesto*, Amsterdam: BIS, 2019.
Goodreads. "The Media Represents a World that Is More Real than Reality", *Goodreads*, https://www.goodreads.com/quotes/7417476-the-media-represents-world-that-is-more-real-than-reality.
Greenberg, Clement. *Art and Culture: Critical Essays*, Boston: Beacon Press, 1989.
Groys, Boris. *In the Flow*, London - New York: Verso, 2016.
Han, Byung-Chul. *Saving Beauty*, tr. Daniel Steuer, Cambridge: Polity, 2018.
Hegel, G. W. F. *Aesthetics: Lectures on Fine Art*, Volume 1, tr. T. M. Knox, Oxford: Oxford University Press, 1975.
Heidegger, Martin. *The Question Concerning Technology*, tr. William Lovitt, New York-London: Harper & Row, 1977.
Higgins, Eliot (@EliotHiggins). Making Pictures of Trump Getting Arrested while Waiting for Trump's Arrest, *Twitter [X]*, 20 March 2023, https://x.com/EliotHiggins/status/1637927681734987777.
______. Meanwhile, in AI Trump World, *Twitter [X]*, 21 March 2023, https://x.com/EliotHiggins/status/1638114034263240704.
______. Apparently Doing a Viral Thread about Donald Trump Using Midjourney, *Twitter [X]*, 22 March 2023, https://x.com/EliotHiggins/status/1638470303310389248.
Hill, Kashmir. The Secretive Company That Might End Privacy as We Know It, *New York Times*, 18 January 2020, https://www.nytimes.com/2020/01/18/technology/clearview-privacy-facial-recognition.html.
Hirst, Damien. *The Currency* [Artwork], HENI, 2021.
Hooper, Tobe (dir.). *The Texas Chain Saw Massacre*, Vortex Inc., 1974.
Hui, Yuk. *Art and Cosmotechnics*, New York: e-flux, 2021.
ISHU. *Signature ISHU Scarf*, 2016, https://theishu.com/products/the-ishu?variant=41949781655575.
Kardashian, Kim (@KimKardashian). What Color Is that Dress?, *X [Twitter]*, 27 February 2015, https://x.com/kimkardashian/status/571168149871177730.
Kittler, Friedrich. *Optical Media: Berlin Lectures 1999*, tr. Anthony Enns, Cambridge: Polity, 2010.
Kusama, Yayoi. *Infinity Mirrored Room - Filled with the Brilliance of Life*

[Artwork], London: Tate, 2011.
Lacan, Jacques. *Seminar XI: The Four Fundamental Concepts of Psychoanalysis*, tr. Alan Sheridan, New York - London: W. W. Norton, 1998.
_____. *Écrits*, tr. Alan Sheridan, London - New York: Routledge, 2001.
Lakoff, George and Johnson, Mark. *Metaphors We Live By*, Chicago - London: University of Chicago Press, 1980.
Lek, Lawrence (dir.). *Sinofuturism (1839 - 2046 AD)*, https://sinofuturism.com/.
Levinas, Emmanuel. *Totality and Infinity*, tr. Alphonso Lingis, The Hague - Boston - London: Martinus Nijhoff, 1979.
Lewis, Kelly. Social Media Platforms Are Complicit in Censoring Palestinian Voices, *The Conversation*, 24 May 2021, https://theconversation.com/social-media-platforms-are-complicit-in-censoring-palestinian-voices-161094.
Lewis, Sarah. The Racial Bias Built Into Photography, *The New York Times*, 25 April 2019, https://www.nytimes.com/2019/04/25/lens/sarah-lewis-racial-bias-photography.html.
Lovink, Geert. Narcissus Confirmed: Technologies of the Minimal Selfie, in Katharina Motyl and Regina Schober (eds) *The Failed Individual: Amid Exclusion, Resistance, and the Pleasure of Non-Conformity* (pp. 347 - 356), Frankfurt - New York: 2017.
_____. *Extinction Internet: Our Inconvenient Moment of Truth*, Amsterdam: Institute of Network Cultures, 2022.
Lunar Princess Strife (@Strife212). AI = Applied Demonology, *X [Twitter]*, 30 April 2020, https://x.com/Strife212/status/1255789106522656773.
Magritte, René. *Not to Be Reproduced* [Artwork], Rotterdam: Museum Boijmans Van Beuningen, 1937.
Mallarmé, Stephan. *The Book*, tr. Sylvia Gorelick, Cambridge: Exact Change, 2018.
Mann, Farhad (dir.). *Max Headroom*, Season 1, Episode 1, ABC, 1987.
McLuhan, Marshall. *Understanding Media: The Extensions of Man*, London - New York: Ark, 1987.
_____. Playboy Interview: "Marshall McLuhan—A Candid Conversation with the High Priest of Popcult and Metaphysician of Media", in Eric McLuhan and Frank Zingrone (eds) *Essential McLuhan* (222 - 260), London: Routledge, 2005.
McLuhan, Marshall and Powers, Bruce R. *The Global Village: Transformations in World Life and Media in the 21st Century*, New York - Oxford: Oxford University Press, 1989.
McLuhan, Marshall and Fiore, Quentin. *The Medium Is the Massage: An Inventory of Effects*, London: Penguin, 1967.
McMullen, Ken (dir.). *Ghost Dance*, Channel Four, 1983.
Meta. Violent and Graphic Content, *Transparency Center*, https://transparency.meta.com/en-gb/policies/community-standards/violent-graphic-content.
Mindless Toys. *methaphone*, 2025, https://mindless-toys.com/products/methaphone-a-mobile-detox-device.
Moore, Gordon. Cramming More Components onto Integrated Circuits, *Electronics Magazine*, *38*(8), 19 April 1965.
Morton, Rocky and Jankel, Annabel (dir.). *Max Headroom: 20 Minutes into the Future*, Channel 4, 1985.
Mulvey, Laura. Visual Pleasure and Narrative Cinema, in Leo Braudy and Marshall Cohen (eds), *Film Theory and Criticism: Introductory Readings* (pp. 833 - 844), New York: Oxford University Press, 1999.

Nietzsche, Friedrich. *The Will to Power*, tr. Walter Kaufmann and R. J. Hollingdale, New York: Vintage, 1968.
_____. *Gay Science: With a Prelude in Rhymes and an Appendix of Songs*, tr. Walter Kaufmann, London: Vintage, 1974.
_____. Twilight of the Idols, in Walter Kaufmann, *The Portable Nietzsche* (pp. 463 – 564), tr. Walter Kaufmann, Middlesex: Penguin Books, 1984.
_____. The Wanderer and His Shadow, in *Human All Too Human: A Book for Free Spirits* (pp. 301 – 395), tr. R. J. Hollingdale, Cambridge: Cambridge University Press, 1996.
_____. *Thus Spoke Zarathustra: A Book for All and None*, tr. Adrian del Caro, Cambridge: Cambridge University Press, 2006.
Nolan, Christopher (dir.). *Interstellar*, Paramount, 2014 (re-release: 2024).
Ovid. *Metamorphoses*, Book III, tr. Brookes More, Boston: Cornhill Publishing Co., 1922.
Plato. Republic, tr. Paul Shorey, in Edith Hamilton and Huntington Cairns (eds) *The Collected Dialogues of Plato. Including the Letters* (pp. 575 – 844), Princeton: Princeton University Press, 1973.
Pliny the Elder. *Natural History*, Book XXXV, tr. Harris Rackman, Cambridge: Loeb, 1938.
Postman, Neil. *Amusing Ourselves to Death: Public Discourse in the Age of Show Business*, York: Metheun, 1987.
Rafman, Jon. *The Nine Eyes of Google Street View* [Photographs], 2008 – present, https://9-eyes.com/.
Raimi, Sam (dir.). *Spider-Man*, Sony, 2002.
Reynolds, Simon. *Retromania: Pop Culture's Addiction to its Own Past*, London: Faber & Faber, 2010.
Russo, Anthony and Russo, Joe (dir.). *Captain America: Civil War*, Marvel Studios, 2016.
Sloterdijk, Peter. "I Am Not a Man, I Am Dynamite": Peter Sloterdijk on Nietzsche, *Los Angeles Review of Books*, 17 May 2018, https://lareviewofbooks.org/entitled-opinions/not-man-dynamite-peter-sloterdijk-nietzsche/.
Smith, Gabriel (@gabriel666smith). Samuel Beckett, It Seems, Was Very Popular in Japan, and Did Many Commercial Endorsements for Japanese Products, *X [Twitter]*, 19 November 2023, https://x.com/gabriel666smith/status/1726667976516993201.
_____. Brat: *A Ghost Story*, London: Penguin, 2024.
Sontag, Susan. *On Photography*, Middlesex: Penguin, 1977.
Steyerl, Hito. *The Wretched of the Screen*, London: Sternberg Press, 2012.
Stiegler, Bernard. *For a New Critique of Political Economy*, tr. Daniel Ross, Cambridge: Polity, 2010.
Tanner, Grafton. *The Hours Have Lost Their Clock: The Politics of Nostalgia*, London: Zer0 Books, 2021.
The Wachowskis (dir.). *The Matrix*, Warner Bros., Village Roadshow Pictures, 1999.
_____. *The Matrix Resurrections*, Warner Bros., Village Roadshow Pictures, 2021.
The Wall Street Journal. How Shein Built a $66B Fast-Fashion Empire | WSJ The Economics Of, *YouTube*, 29 November 2023, https://www.youtube.com/watch?v=gWotBPtsulo.
Torres, Chris. *Nyan Cat* [Artwork], Foundation, 2021.
von Clausewitz, Carl. *On War*, tr. Michael Howard and Peter Paret, Oxford:

Oxford University Press, 2007.
Wark, McKenzie. My Collectible Ass, *e-flux*, 85, 2017, https://www.e-flux.com/journal/85/156418/my-collectible-ass/.
Wong, Julia Carrie. The Viral Selfie App ImageNet Roulette Seemed Fun – Until it Called Me a Racist Slur, *The Guardian*, 18 September 2019, https://www.theguardian.com/technology/2019/sep/17/imagenet-roulette-asian-racist-slur-selfie.

List of figures

Figure 1. Samuel Beckett and King Bowser, created by Gabriel Smith, 2023, available at https://x.com/gabriel666smith/status/1726667976516993201.
Figure 2. Moore's law, created by shigeru23, 2011, source: http://pc.watch.impress.co.jp/docs/column/, licensed under CC BY-SA 3.0 (https://creativecommons.org/licenses/by-sa/3.0/deed.en), availabe at https://commons.wikimedia.org/wiki/File:Moores_law_(1970-2011).PNG.
Figure 3. A person dressed as Pepe the Frog, a character known from Internet memes, created by Tomasz Molina, 2022, licensed under CC BY-SA 4.0 (https://creativecommons.org/licenses/by-sa/4.0/deed.en), available at https://commons.wikimedia.org/wiki/File:Pyrkon_2022_-_Pepe_the_Frog.jpg.
Figure 4. Garbage dump, created by Mussi Katz, 2022, available at https://commons.wikimedia.org/wiki/File:Quibdo_Garbage_dump.jpg.
Figure 5. Hand cursor (cropped from original image with arrow cursor), created by Lordalpha1, 2010, licensed under CC BY 2.5 (https://creativecommons.org/licenses/by/2.5/deed.en), available at https://commons.wikimedia.org/wiki/File:Mouse-cursor-hand-pointer.svg.
Figure 6. iPhone 8, created by Rafael Fernandez, 2017, licensed under CC BY-SA 4.0 (see link above), available at https://commons.wikimedia.org/wiki/File:iPhone_8_vector.svg.
Figure 7. "Salmon swimming in the river" prompt.
Figure 8. Mona Lisa with ImageNet Roulette label.
Figure 9. Mona Lisa with DeepDream effect using VGG16 network trained on ImageNet, created by P. J. Finlay, 2021, source: https://github.com/PJ-Finlay/pytorch-deepdream, available at https://commons.wikimedia.org/wiki/File:%22Mona_Lisa%22_with_DeepDream_effect_using_VGG16_network_trained_on_ImageNet.jpg.
Figures 10. The first image of Sagittarius A*, the supermassive black hole at the center of the Milky Way, created by EHT Collaboration, 2022, CC BY 4.0 (see link above), available at https://commons.wikimedia.org/wiki/File:EHT_Saggitarius_A_black_hole.tif.
Figure 11. DJI Phantom 4K drone in action, created by Suyash Dwivedi, 2019, licensed under CC BY-SA 4.0 (see link above), available at https://commons.wikimedia.org/wiki/File:DJI_Phantom_4K_drone_in_action.jpg.
Figure 12. Altair 8800 advertisement in the May 1976 issue of BYTE magazine, created by MITS staff, 1976, available at https://commons.wikimedia.org/wiki/File:Altair_Computer_Ad_May_1976.jpg.
Figure 13. Max Headroom broadcast signal intrusion, 1987, available at https://commons.wikimedia.org/wiki/File:Max_Headroom_broadcast_signal_intrusion.jpg.
Figure 14. Seal of Solomon, 2008, available at https://commons.wikimedia.org/wiki/File:Goetia_seal_of_solomon.svg.
Figure 15. Printed circuit board design, created by Felipe Sanches, 2008, licensed under CC BY-SA 2.0 (see link above), available at https://commons.wikimedia.org/wiki/File:PARTYland_Remake_-_Jan_8th_2008_-_PCB_layout_-_lamp_control_board_(2176523765).png.
Figure 16. Bliss, the default Windows XP wallpaper, used with permission from Microsoft, 2017, available at https://en.wikipedia.org/wiki/File:Bliss_(Windows_XP).png.
Figure 17. Panda Head meme, created by Akanosuke666, 2024, licensder under CC BY-SA 3.0 (see link above), available at https://funkin-fanon.fandom.com/wiki/VS._Chinese_Panda_Meme.
Figures 18 - 19. Paris Hilton wearing signature ISHU scarf, created by ISHU,

2016, available at https://theishu.com/products/the-ishu.
Figure 20. Black square edited over a Black Lives Matter protest of police brutality in the rotunda of the Mall of America in Bloomington, created by Nicholas Upton, 2014, source: https://www.flickr.com/photos/47379772@N03/15879284388/, licensed under the CC BY-SA 2.0 (https://creativecommons.org/licenses/by-sa/2.0/deed.en), available at https://en.wikipedia.org/wiki/File:Black_Lives_Matter_protest,_Mall_of_America,_December_2014.jpg.
Figure 21. Trump's arrest, created by Eliot Higgins, 2023, source: https://twitter.com/EliotHiggins/status/1637927681734987777, available at https://commons.wikimedia.org/wiki/File:Trump%E2%80%99s_arrest_(1).jpg.
Figure 22. All Eyes on Rafah, created by Amirul Shah and Zila Abka, 2024, source: https://www.greaterkashmir.com/latest-news/all-eyes-on-rafah-why-ai-generated-image-is-trending-on-social-media/, available at https://commons.wikimedia.org/wiki/File:All_Eyes_On_Rafah.webp.
Figure 23. Watermelon logo, created by RDSRichy, 2021, CC BY-SA 4.0 (https://creativecommons.org/licenses/by-sa/4.0/deed.en), available at https://en.wikipedia.org/wiki/File:Watermelon_logo.png.
Figure 24. Firefighting operation on the Pine Gulch Fire in Colorado, United States, created by Kyle Miller (Wyoming Hotshots/USFS), 2020, available at https://commons.wikimedia.org/wiki/File:Pine_Gulch_Fire_(9406).jpg.
Figure 25. Sad emoji from the Twemoji project, created by Twitter, source: https://github.com/twitter/twemoji/, 2014 - 2022, licensed under CC BY 4.0 (see link above), available at https://commons.wikimedia.org/wiki/File:Twemoji12_1f625.svg.
Figure 26. No image, created by Yoyon Pujiyono, 2021, licensed under CC BY 4.0 (see link above), available at https://commons.wikimedia.org/wiki/File:No_Image_(2879926)_-_The_Noun_Project.svg.

Colophon

Set Margins' #86
Beyond the Image
On Visual Culture in the Twenty-First Century
By Alessandro Sbordoni

ISBN: 978-90-836052-3-4
Editor: Alessandro Sbordoni
Graphic design: Freek Lomme
Text editor: Alessandro Sbordoni
Proofreader: Alessandro Sbordoni, Sam Woolfe
Printer: ...
Font: LiSong Pro Light

Made possible thanks to the generous support of Freek Lomme and Alessandro Sbordoni

First edition, 2025

Set Margins'
www.setmargins.press